Beginning Songwriter's Answer Book

BEGINNING SONGWRITER'S ANSWER BOOK

PAUL ZOLLO

Writer's
Digest
Books

Cincinnati, Ohio

The National Academy of Songwriters is a nonprofit organization designed to inform and protect songwriters. For more information, write to:
The National Academy of Songwriters
6381 Hollywood Blvd., Suite 780
Hollywood, CA 90028
Or call 213/463-7178 (or 1-800-826-7287 toll free outside California).

Beginning Songwriter's Answer Book. Copyright © 1990 by Paul Zollo. Printed and bound in the United States of America. All rights reserved. No part of this book may be reproduced in any form or by any electronic or mechanical means including information storage and retrieval systems without permission in writing from the publisher, except by a reviewer, who may quote brief passages in a review. Published by Writer's Digest Books, an imprint of F&W Publications, Inc., 1507 Dana Ave., Cincinnati, Ohio 45207. First edition.

94 93 92 91 90   5 4 3 2 1

Library of Congress Cataloging-in-Publication Data

Zollo, Paul
    Beginning songwriter's answer book / by Paul Zollo
        p.   cm.
    ISBN 0-89879-393-9
    1. Popular music—Writing and publishing. I. Title.
MT67.Z57   1990
782.42164'03—dc20   90-31301
                                                                CIP
                                                                MN

Design by Joan Jacobus.
Music engravings by William Holab, New York.

For Leslie
for putting up with me.

Ignore everybody else and do what you feel.
—Loudon Wainwright III

Contents

$\triangledown$

Acknowledgments

Special thanks to my parents, who encouraged me from the start to be a songwriter, and to my brothers and sisters for always being there to listen to my new songs.

I'd also like to thank the following people without whom this book never could have been written: Steve Schalchlin, Dan Kirkpatrick, Julie Whaley, Bill Holab, Scott Eyerly, Mark Spier, Tom Bowden, Paul Simon, Joe Borja, Bob Dylan, Tom Waits, Shirley Bennett, Al Schlesinger, Daniel Woodington, EJ Doyle, Mike Greene, Hollywood Sheet Music, Kevin Odegard, Jean Farmer, Sean Heaney, Lucy Hagan, Purlie Olloz, Verno Urquiza, Camille Bertagnolli, Judd Sager, George Burakowski and everyone at the National Academy of Songwriters. Many thanks to all.

Thanks, too, to the many songwriters I was lucky enough to interview for *SongTalk* and whose wisdom I have used in these pages: Randy Newman, Lamont Dozier, Van Dyke Parks, Rickie Lee Jones, Pete Seeger, Loudon Wainwright, Willie Dixon, Jimmy Webb, Livingston & Evans, Carole King, Todd Rundgren and Frank Zappa. Thank you all for sharing so much.

Preface

I have to admit I felt a certain bit of reluctance when Julie Whaley of Writer's Digest Books suggested to me that we do a book called *Beginning Songwriter's Answer Book*. The roots of this reluctance lay in my feelings that there are no real answers when it comes to songwriting; it's a mysterious, spiritual and often ambiguous pursuit. Sure, there are definite answers about the business issues: royalties, copyrights, etc. But when it comes to the question of how to write songs, I certainly didn't feel that I was in any position to offer answers.

For the past couple years, in the midst of writing my own songs, recording and performing with my band, I've been making my living not by answering questions but by asking them. As the editor of *SongTalk*, the journal of the National Academy of Songwriters, I've been in the supremely privileged position of interviewing many of our world's most accomplished and influential songwriters. These interviews were conducted with a specific concentration on the creation of songs, and I was asking these questions as much for my personal knowledge as for that of all my readers. I've always felt that it's beneficial for a songwriter to read the ways of the greats, those songwriters who have moved the world with their words and music.

So I was pleased and persuaded to write this book when Julie told me it would be acceptable to include portions of many of these interviews in the answers of the book. In this way, different sides of the issues that arise in the following pages are explored through the use of the often conflicting opinions of these songwriters.

When Johnny Mercer and Harold Arlen wrote "That Old Black Magic," people said, "You can't do that! It's too long." The song has a 64-bar melody which was considered far too long at the time. Mercer and Arlen had the wisdom to know that their song was right and they left it unchanged. It went on to become a standard and has been recorded hundreds of times.

Experiences like these teach us that anytime someone sets down rules about songwriting, new songs come along to break them. Hopefully this book will reinforce the understanding that there are no easy answers to most questions about songwriting, there are only opinions. The following contains an abundance of these opinions: mine as well as those of others.

Lyrics

▼ *As a lyricist, is it important for me to read a lot?*

Yes. Read as much as you can. Read fiction, nonfiction, poetry, whatever you can get your hands on. Because one-half of a song is made up of words, you want to be as experienced with words as possible. And reading is simply a way of putting fuel into your tank.

Any writer should strive to be as literate as possible and the lyricist is no exception. There are too many lyricists writing songs today without much mastery of the language. The best way to gain this mastery is by doing it, first of all, but also by reading and experiencing the way great writers use the language.

Also, reading enables a songwriter to get in touch with subject matter that you don't encounter in your own life. For example, I have a song about a religious crusade in the Deep South, something I have no firsthand experience of at all, but I've read a wonderful novel that deals with the subject and made me see the symbolic potential of it.

Randy Newman told *SongTalk* that reading has helped him: "It enabled me not to have to live, because I can read," he joked. But there's a lot of truth in that. Though Randy hasn't been to Africa, he wrote a powerful song about that part of the world called "Christmas in Capetown." His experience of Africa was gained by reading Nadine Gordimer's books on the subject.

Bruce Springsteen, after releasing his darkly beautiful *Nebraska* album, said in an interview that he was highly influenced by the stories of the writer William Price Fox. He mentioned how Fox's use of telling details enabled him to delve into the details of the stories he wove himself on that album.

Bruce Hornsby, in *SongTalk*, discussed the huge influence of Southern literature on his life, including the books of William Styron, Lee Smith, and William Hoffman. And this southern influence is clearly reflected in his work.

A knowledge of myths and ancient tales can be of great benefit to songwriters. Myths have survived for ages precisely because of the strength and timelessness of their messages. Knowledge of all myths from all cultures can add a great resonance to your work, as you can utilize the timeless symbols and icons that poets have been using throughout the centuries. And these old myths will shed new light on today's world.

Knowledge of the Bible—both the Old and the New Testaments is highly valuable for the songwriter, both for the beauty of the language therein and also to become familiar with all the symbols contained in those pages, which are the most powerful parables Western man knows. Whether or not your own personal faith includes believing in any of these stories, their mythical power cannot be denied.

One of the reasons Bob Dylan's work still resonates many years after it was written has to do with his abundant usage of these ancient symbols.

If you went through all of his songs and looked only for biblical imagery and references to the Bible, you'd be amazed by their prevalence. (And I'm referring to work long before his so-called "born-again" stage.)

Let's look at one of these songs, "All Along the Watchtower," (a classic version of which was recorded by Jimi Hendrix). Here is the final verse:

> *All along the watchtower, princes kept the view*
> *Two riders were approaching, the wind began to*
> *   howl . . .*

Now let's look at a passage from the Old Testament, Isaiah 21:6-9:

> *. . . the Lord said, Go set a watchman, let him announce what he sees, when he sees riders, horsemen in pairs . . . Then he who saw cried, Upon a watchtower I stand, O Lord . . . and here they come, horsemen in pairs . . . Fallen, fallen is Babylon; and all the images of her gods. . . .*

Of course, Dylan ties in the stories of the Bible with other myths from a variety of ancient sources, including the Tarot. These are sources that are, according to Dylanologist Aidan Day in his book *Jokerman*, "rich in psychological implication."

Some say that we are what we eat. Writers are what they read. The more delving you do into the literature of the past, the more depth your songs will possess. Sometimes, when searching one's own mind for the right lyric, it seems as if we've gone to the well too many times and there's nothing left to draw from. Reading can fill up that well with a wealth of images, symbols, myths, and ideas that you can then apply to your own life and to the lives of those around you.

▼ Is it a good idea to collect phrases and ideas for songs even when not working on a specific song?

Yes. One of the puzzles that a songwriter has to solve is how to put together disparate parts. So if you come across an interesting line or phrase, even if you don't have a song to put it in at the time, write it down, save it, and maybe it will come in handy at a later time. Even if you don't have any idea how it might be used you might find that a future song you are working on will need an inter-

esting phrase, and this might be just the one to set you off on a new direction.

It's a good idea to start a notebook in which you can keep these phrases. Many songwriters write down ideas and phrases on scraps of paper which are easy to lose. So if you have a main notebook for your ideas, it makes it easier to stay organized.

An even better method for saving phrases and ideas is to use a computer. If you have one, it can be an ideal tool for saving and storing these fragments. You can have a file for song ideas in which you can store whatever song concepts you might come up with.

▼ How about titles? Should I also collect potential song titles?

Yes. Most songwriters who keep their ears perked catch potential titles going by. Often a good title can serve as an excellent starting point for an entire song concept. While you can write a great song based on a title that's already been used, it's not easy to do. Bruce Springsteen has pulled it off a number of times. "Dancing in the Dark" is a well-known standard (by Howard Dietz & Arthur Schwartz) and yet Springsteen was able to make the title completely his own in his hit of the same name. And at times he has even expanded on titles; "Walk Like a Man" is a title Chuck Berry first used, yet Springsteen uses it in a hauntingly revealing way in the song he wrote from his *Tunnel of Love* album.

But few writers are like Springsteen, able to express so much emotion in so few words. It's a better idea to find your own title, a title no one has ever used before.

A song I wrote with an unusual title is called "Archeology of Illinois." I came across that title while visiting my hometown, Chicago, and leafing through a catalog from an adult education program. "Archeology of Illinois" was the name of one of the courses they offered. When I saw it I knew its potential instantly, seeing it as a way of dealing with the suburbanization of the wilderness as well as the previous history of the land, the Indians that once lived in the area. Finding that one title set me off writing a song I had not ever considered writing before. So I would encourage beginning writers to stay on the lookout for interesting titles around which entire songs can be written.

Many songwriters have told tales of finding titles in unusual places. Paul Simon admitted to finding the title to "Mother and Child Reunion" in a Chinese restaurant. It was the name of a dish that had chicken and eggs together. The Beatles' "Being for the Benefit of Mr. Kite!" was taken straight off a circus poster that John Lennon discovered. "Helter Skelter" was the name of a carnival ride in England that Paul McCartney enjoyed. "Where Have All the Flowers Gone?" by Pete Seeger was found in a Ukrainian poem. "Seventh Son" by Willie Dixon is from the Bible.

But finding an unusual title is not enough. You also have to see in it the potential for a song, and then carry it through and build a whole song around the title that flows as effortlessly as if the song was written from the beginning to the end. Every line of "Being for the Benefit of Mr. Kite!" for example, is at home in the circuslike atmosphere Lennon creates; the title must be presented in a world where it doesn't stand out but where it makes sense and belongs, as in the following:

> For the benefit of Mr. Kite, there will be a show tonight on trampoline
> The Hendersons will all be there, Late of Pablo Fanques Fair—what a scene
> Over men and horses hoops and garters
> Lastly through a hogshead of real fire!

Paul Simon is a great songwriter because he can find a title like "Rene and Georgette Magritte with Their Dog after the War" (which he found in a book of photographs) and make a song out of it that works. You have to make sure the lyrics are as colorful as the title itself. To have a whole set of recycled, pedestrian lyrics matched to an unusual title only emphasizes the paucity of content in the lyrics.

▼ What other kinds of fragments should I try to save?

Look for idioms, or conversational turns of speech, that are common and yet can be used in a song in a new way. A great thing about songs is that they take our common language and reflect it to us in a new light, amplified by music and rhythm and rhyme. You can take what is a fairly ordinary and frequently heard phrase, such as "still crazy after all these years" or "with a little help from my friends" or "something in the way she moves" and fit it into a song so that we hear it in a new way, or many new ways. You can take a phrase such as "I blinked once and it was gone," as Steve Forbert has done in the song "I Blinked Once," and present it on many different levels. He applies the phrase first to a day, then a whole decade (the seventies), and then to a person's entire lifetime. The same phrase takes on different meanings due to the context in which it is used.

"It's kind of a Chuck Berry style," Forbert told SongTalk, "in which you make the same points with the verse but you use different examples. 'Too Much Monkey Business' by Chuck Berry would be a case in point, where you make the same point with each verse but with each one you expand on it. 'I Blinked Once' kept getting more serious with each verse and that's what I wanted to do."

▼ Where do I find these phrases, fragments, titles, and idioms?

Everywhere. You have to keep your eyes and your ears open. You can get them from reading: the newspaper is an excellent place in which to come in contact with innumerable strange and interesting turns of speech. The new words and phrases coined to describe current calamities are always contained in a paper, as are countless potential song concepts. Woody Guthrie was known to write several songs a day straight out of the newspaper.

Poetry is an obvious place to look, as poets have already bent the language in new ways to present new meanings we may have been unaware of.

As a songwriter, you can even take advantage of time spent at bus or subway stops, in buses and trains, in restaurants, etc., where you can overhear people talking. This is a great source of conversational language: not just the words but the way people use them in everyday speech, as well as the slang and lingo that people use. As an exercise, next time you are on a bus or in similar surroundings, jot down all the extraneous bits of conversation you hear, regardless of their meaning. Later you can read it as a free-verse poem, and you may be amazed by what you collect; see if you can use any of it in a song lyric.

TV and radio talk shows, such as Larry King, Oprah Winfrey, and Donahue, are surprisingly good places to hear the way people use the language, as well as the ideas on their minds. Watch one of these shows and listen to the way people actually speak, and write down interesting phrases or fragments for later use. Then write a song in which you use as many of these phrases as you can. This can be a good way to discover new juxtapositions: putting together imagery that might seem incongruous at first but which can prove to be powerful in the right setting.

▼ *Is it a good idea to do research for song lyrics?*

If you are working on songs for a musical about a historical personage, research is a necessity to ensure accuracy. Songwriters working on songs apart from any musical or movie rarely do research, and yet it can open doors to amazing subjects and ideas you never would have come up with on your own.

Consider these two examples of songs about famous people who lived in the past, neither of which could have been written with as much love and potency without some knowledge of the subject. The first song is Don McLean's "Vincent" (from *American Pie*), a song that numerous songwriters, including Randy Newman and Janis Ian, have praised for its greatness. That greatness stems not only from the specificities about Van Gogh, but also from the universal nature of the song: "and so you took your life as lovers often do/this world was never meant for one as beautiful as you ... " McLean brilliantly weaves the story of the artist with the story of all artists and all feeling people, and puts this to a gorgeous melody wedded perfectly to the visual immediacy of such lines as the opening, referring to the painting: "Starry starry night ... " The power of such a song, which uses the real life of an actual person as a symbol, is tremendous.

Joni Mitchell uses the same technique in her song about Amelia Earhart, "Amelia" (from *Hejira*). She takes the mysterious tale of the famous flyer and uses it as a starting point for a song about her own journeys and about the danger of getting lost and never found: "A ghost of aviation/she was swallowed by the sky/Or by the sea, like me she had a dream to fly/Like Icarus ascending/On beautiful foolish arms/Amelia, it was just a false alarm. . . ."

Notice how in a song about one mythical figure she refers to another from a much older myth, Daedalus and Icarus. When Icarus flew too close to the sun with his wings of wax and feathers, the wax melted and he fell to the earth. Joni's knowledge of this mythology adds another level to the Amelia mystery, which in turn refers to her own life.

Research can also enable you to find new themes about which to center your song. To the best of my knowledge, nobody ever wrote a song about Van Gogh before. Yet after hearing Don McLean's song, it seems like such an obvious and ideal choice. There is a world of content that rarely makes it into most pop or rock songs. Certain songwriters have stretched the limits of what a song can express and contain, but many are content to stay within parameters others have set. Sure, there's always a place for a good love song. But so many have been written already, it's hard to write one with anything new in it.

As a creative challenge to yourself, write a song with a content and with words that you've never used before. This will quickly reveal to you the limit of what you consider to be an acceptable song lyric. See if you can break out of those constraints and express yourself in new ways. In this way, songwriting is a means of self-discovery as well; you come to realize what symbols are the most meaningful for you as well as those words and symbols that clash with your sensibilities. Don't settle for something because somebody else has used it in a song: find your own way of expressing yourself in song.

▼ *What is a rhyme?*

The word "rhyme," according to Webster, is a noun that means "a correspondence in terminal sounds of two or more words, lines of verse, or other units of composition." In simpler terms, a rhyme occurs when two words match in every way except for the letter (or letters) they begin with. A rhyme for the word "sky" is "die." Other rhymes are "eye," "my," "fly," and "try."

The beauty of rhymes lies in the way they connect lines, phrases, and ideas. Rhymes can put thoughts into a memorable order, so that throughout history—even prior to the time of the printing press—rhymes have been utilized to help people remember key facts. For example, the calendar: "Thirty days has September, April, June, and November . . ." Or wisdom about the weather: "Red sky at night, shepherd's delight/red sky at morning, shepherds take warning." In the same way, songwriters can use rhymes to beautifully connect and combine lines of our langauge, so that, rather than tell us about the calendar or the weather, Ira Gershwin can tell us about the timelessness of love in "Love Is Here to Stay":

> It's very clear our love is here to stay
> Not for a year but ever and a day . . .

▼ What is a false rhyme?

A false rhyme, also known as an assonant rhyme, is an almost-rhyme, the opposite of a true rhyme. It's a "rhyme" in which two words match in terms of their vowel sounds but not their consonants.

For example, a true rhyme for the word "rain" is "pain." It's a true rhyme because both the vowel sound (the long *a*) and the consonant at the end of the word (the *n*) match. A *false rhyme* for the word "rain" is "game" because although the vowel sound (the long *a*) matches in both words, the consonants do not match: "rain" ends with an *n* while "game" ends with the sound of an *m*. So the words are very close and do present a partial but incomplete rhyme, hence, a false rhyme.

▼ Is it okay to use false rhymes in songs?

Again, there are no rules. While you can often get away with using false rhymes, I would suggest that you use them sparingly. A false rhyme in a prominent position—such as to set up the title line—can be distracting. Though false rhymes have been used in countless songs, even those written by the finest writers, they can make a song seem amateurish and even sloppy to a publisher.

Sure, Bob Dylan can get away with it in a song like "Shelter from the Storm" in which he rhymes "storm" with "thorns," "morn," "horn," and other false rhymes, but Dylan is Dylan, an established artist who doesn't need to make an impression on a publisher. When writing songs to take to publishers, the writer should strive to make them as seamless and professional as possible. Using true rhymes is one way of doing this.

It should be mentioned that some songwriters disagree with the feeling that false rhymes should be avoided, suggesting that the meaning of the song is more crucial than the perfection of a rhyme scheme. One interviewer complained to Jackson Browne about using false rhymes on a new album, saying that Jackson was one of the few remaining songwriters who could be counted on to rhyme "world" with "unfurled." Jackson answered that you can only use a word like "unfurled" so many times, and there comes a point in your writing when you care more about meaning and less about cleverness.

In songwriting, it's the way all the parts add up that matter. While I may have suffered at times from trying too hard for a perfect rhyme and not hard enough to make the words work in context, the songs that ultimately work the best are the ones that do both: have a clear, clean rhyme structure and lines that flow naturally in context and meaning. These are the magical songs, the ones in which it seems as if no other line could possibly be used.

▼ What is an inner rhyme?

And inner rhyme is a rhyme that occurs within a line instead of at the end of a line. For example, the opening of Gershwin's classic, "Love Is Here to Stay": "It's very clear our love is here to stay/Not for a year but ever and a day . . ." The inner rhymes are "clear," "here," and "year." The outer rhymes are "stay" and "day." The inner rhyme is a traditional songwriting technique used abundantly by previous generations of songwriters and less frequently today. Yet its use can add a musicality and beauty to your lyrics that is hard to match.

▼ What is a rhyme scheme?

A rhyme scheme is a repeating pattern for the rhymes in a song. A common rhyme scheme for a quatrain (or four-line section) is an ABCB pattern. Each letter name refers to a line of the quatrain. When a letter repeats, as the B does, that is where the rhyme occurs. In an ABCB pattern, the rhyme falls where the B is, on the second and fourth line. Once you establish a rhyme scheme, the pattern must repeat in each quatrain. An example of an ABCB pattern is this famous refrain from "September Song." The music is by Kurt Weill and the lyrics by Maxwell Anderson:

> *It's a long long while (A)*
> *From May to December (B)*
> *But the days grow short (C)*
> *When you reach September (B)*

▼ What is an ABAB rhyme scheme?

If the rhyme scheme for a quatrain is ABAB, it means that you have interlocking rhymes. Instead of having two lines that rhyme and two lines that don't, every line has a matching rhyme. The first and third lines rhyme as do the second and fourth lines. This is a tough rhyme scheme to pull off. To use it in a natural, unforced way takes some mastery of rhymes, as in this example from Bob Dylan's ode to his former wife, "Sara," from his album *Desire*:

> *Now the beach is deserted except for some kelp*
> *And a piece of an old ship that lies on the shore.*
> *You always responded when I needed your help*
> *You gave me a map and a key to your door*

Methods of Rhyming

To write in this rhyme scheme effectively, or any rhyme scheme for that matter, it's sometimes necessary to work backwards, coming up with the last rhymes first and then figuring out setups for them. In the previous example, that would mean coming up with the lines: "You always responded when I needed your help/You gave me a map and a key to your door." Then you work backwards to figure out preceding lines that will seem unobtrusive and which will set up the rhyme.

It's a good idea when rhyming to have the weaker of two rhymes come first in the song. By using this method of working backwards, you can set up a strong line with a slightly weaker one (we never want lines that are too weak, of course; weak is meant in a relative sense). If you have the strong line first and the weak line second, it's obvious that it is there because it's a rhyme and not because it belongs to the context of the song.

This method is especially useful when writing in the verse/chorus form and having to set up the title at the end of each verse. Gershwin's marvelous "Love Is Here to Stay" ends with this phrase: "The Rockies may crumble, Gibraltar may tumble/ They're only made of clay, but our love is here to stay." With the title already established, Ira Gershwin had to work backwards, in a sense, to come up with a setup word for "stay." The use of the word "clay" is rather unusual in a love song—how many can you think of with the word "clay" involved? It's a rather bizarre word choice, yet it works beautifully in the context of the song. It's an example of the weaker rhyme coming first; the use of the word "clay" is acceptable because it sets up the title, the strongest rhyme in the entire song. Can you imagine, though, how strange it would sound if the lines were reversed, with the weaker rhyme second? We would have something along the lines of "our love is here to stay, longer than the mountains/that are made of clay." The entire emphasis of the line is lost, and the rhyme seems forced. So by always having the weaker rhyme first, setting up a stronger rhyme, you create a sense of inevitability without drawing attention to the rhyme itself.

A rhyme scheme can, of course, apply to any section of a song, even if it is not a quatrain. For example, the six lines of one verse from Dylan's "It's Alright, Ma (I'm Only Bleeding)" end with noon, spoon, balloon, moon, soon, and trying. This is an unusual rhyme scheme in which the first five lines of the verse rhyme and the sixth line rhymes with the sixth line of the next verse. This pattern would be written this way: AAAAAB.

As an exercise, try writing down the rhyme schemes to some of your favorite songs, or even to some of your own songs. Then try to write lyrics in the rhyme schemes that you discover, and see if you can come up with rhymes that feel fresh and unforced. Work backwards if you need to, finding a strong line first and then thinking of a setup line to precede it.

▼ Is it necessary for my songs to rhyme?

While many good songs have been written (for specific reasons) without a real rhyme scheme, most songs require a rhyme pattern or they simply don't sound right. Understand that for ages our ears have been conditioned to expect rhymes at the end of metered verses. If a rhyme doesn't fall where the ear expects it to, the song sounds amateurish.

There have been exceptions—wonderful songs that have no rhymes at all. An example is Paul Simon's beautiful "America," (from Simon and Garfunkel's *Bookends* album). One of the reasons the song works so well even without rhymes is that it is loaded with specific details, creating images so vivid that the lack of rhymes is barely noticed.

Stephen Sondheim said that he will write songs with strict rhyme schemes for characters in musicals who have logical, reasonable ways of thinking, and songs with less strict to no rhyme schemes for characters who are not logical and for whom singing in rhyme would seem wrong. Similarly, in some of Randy Newman's character songs, there are no normal rhyme schemes in songs sung by characters in a conversational manner, as people never normally speak in rhyme and Newman is attempting to capture the essence of actual language as it is spoken.

But these are rare examples that apply only to songs written from a character's point of view. An average song does require a rhyme scheme for aesthetic reasons (it would just sound wrong without one), and also because your song, if you want it published, has to appear professional. Publishers don't need much more than a poor rhyme scheme, or a nonexistent one, to deem your song unprofessional.

In his interview with *SongTalk*, Steve Forbert explained why a rhyme scheme is necessary: "I think the order of it gives a person a feeling of security that is pleasant . . . Because you set it up: 'I'm going away, baby, and I won't be back till fall.' It sets up anticipation, right? 'And if I find me a good loving woman, child, I do believe I won't be

back at all.' In your mind you feel a sense of release and order there because you were anticipating and then you were rewarded with the rhyme. And that's why rhymes have stood the test of time and remain essential."

There are a few better ways of making a point in a song, or of emphasizing your title, than the use of a rhyme scheme. And when a rhyme can be utilized in a natural, unforced way, its power can be great. Let's look at these lines of Bob Dylan's song "I Shall Be Released":

I see my light come shining from the west unto the east
Any day now, any day now I shall be released.

Notice that the title comes in the fourth and final line of the chorus, set up by the use of the word "east" in the second line: "from the west unto the east." The important thing to note is that the setup rhyme, the rhyme that makes the presentation of the title line seem inevitable, fits perfectly into the context of the song.

Dylan is a master at this technique, setting up rhymes in a way that makes it seem that the line couldn't be any other way. And this is what you want to accomplish: no line should draw attention to itself; no line should seem to be in place only to set up a rhyme. So when working on a chorus, for example, that ends in a rhyme, make sure the rhyme is set up by a line that fits both with the rhyme scheme and the meaning of the song.

Dylan has written other songs in which the rhyming is not as masterful and the setups are more obvious. Some of these setups, though, do seem to provide him with interesting content material, however strange. Here's a section from his song, "When I Paint My Masterpiece": "Got to hurry on back to my hotel room/Where I've got me a date with Botticelli's niece/She promised that she'd be right there with me/When I Paint My Masterpiece . . ."

Now you might or might not enjoy the usage of "Botticelli's niece," but either way you can see that it is an unusual setup for the "masterpiece" rhyme and draws attention to itself. You should strive to set up rhymes in a way that is subtle so that the setup line works in the context of the song and fits in with the lines before and after it. Here's another example from Dylan of an effortless setup, this one from a song in the verse/bridge structure in which the title phrase ("Highway 61") requires a different setup each time it is used in the song, "Highway 61 Revisited." One verse ends this way:

> *The next time you see me comin' you better run*
> *Well Abe says, "Where do you want this killing*
> *   done?"*
> *God says, "Out on Highway 61."*

In this example, the title phrase is set up by not one but two rhymes: "run" and "done." Not only that, but the lines flow conversationally and are even presented in a dialogue form between God and Abraham. When you hear the two lines that precede the title line, they do not stand out; there's no clue that they are setups for the final rhyme, although they are. It is this kind of effortless rhyming and rhyme setup that you should strive to accomplish in your writing.

▼ Is it a good idea to use a rhyming dictionary when writing lyrics?

This is an area of disagreement among songwriters. While some of the most gifted wordsmiths in the world, such as Stephen Sondheim, admit their reliance on rhyming dictionaries, others feel that it's cheating to use one, that a good songwriter can invent his own rhymes without the use of a book.

The only real cheating in songwriting is plagiarism; using a book to give you a list of potential rhymes is not cheating in that it won't help you work a word into a song, nor will it help you choose the most suitable rhyme. That is still the job of the writer. Sondheim reasoned that no songwriter should be expected to always have at his fingertips every possible rhyme for the word "askew," for example, when a rhyming dictionary can provide them for you. Coming from him, that should be enough of an endorsement for any songwriter who cares about quality lyrics, as Sondheim has been writing them steadily for decades.

If you do decide to get a rhyming dictionary, look at it closely before you make your purchase to make sure it works well for you. With some of the books I have tried, it took longer to find a rhyme than it would to think up one by myself. And others simply had an incomplete selection of rhymes,

omitting some of the most creative ones while including every pedestrian, overused rhyme there is.

▼ Some lyricists have said that they use a regular dictionary when working. Is this a good idea?

Both a dictionary and a thesaurus can be of great use to a songwriter working on lyrics. Many word processing programs on computers now have built-in dictionaries and thesauruses, so if you write with a computer (as more people do every day), you have instant access.

Using both a dictionary and a thesaurus is helpful because sometimes when working on a lyric you might have an inner sense that a certain word is needed and not be able to find it. Having a whole book of words in front of you is a good way to get that flow going, and even if you don't find the one word you are driving toward, it might suggest others for you.

A dictionary also comes in handy when you are working on alliterative lines. These are lines that are connected not only by rhymes but by words that begin with the same letter, creating a musical flow to the words. For example, this line from Paul Simon's "Boy in the Bubble" (from *Graceland*) which is alliterative both with words that start with *m* and words that start with *b*: ". . . medicine is magical and magical is art/The Boy in the Bubble and the baby with the baboon heart . . ." There are other instances of alliteration in this song as well.

You can use a dictionary to help you find alliterative matches to words. If the words you need all start with the letter *p*, for example, look in the *P*s for a list of every word that begins with this letter. And some of the words will, as I have found, suggest new directions for you to take in the lyrics.

Dictionaries are also helpful to make sure that your word usage is accurate. Often when you're working on a line, the very sounds you are playing with will suggest word choices. With a dictionary, you can quickly check on the definition of the word to make sure it fits your intended meaning.

Also, a dictionary helps one get the spelling of words correct, something even gifted songwriters can use. Few things look as bad to a publisher as songwriters who cannot spell the lyrics of their own song correctly.

▼ *Some people have heard my songs and they liked them, but they said I needed to use more imagery. What do they mean by imagery?*

Imagery is the presentation of images, or pictures, in language. When the word is used in terms of songwriting, it refers to the pictures a songwriter presents in his songs. For example, let's look at this verse from Tom Waits' song "Broken Bicycles":

Broken bicycles, old rusted chains
Rusted handlebars out in the rain . . .

In this song, Waits doesn't state his own feelings, or any emotions for that matter. Instead, he provides *images* and in this way he allows the listener to feel his own emotions, based on each listener's personal associations with that image. "Broken bicycles" represents sadness; that which was once full of life and fun and is now rusting and discarded. While I don't think anyone would find this imagery to be happy, how sad it is depends on one's own associations. This means that no two people will experience your song in the same way; each will respond based on his or her own associations with the images you choose. It's the job of the songwriter, then, to provide images that are vivid and specific enough to evoke an emotional response.

Images allow you to bypass your listeners' intellect and connect directly to their heart. It's like stating a color: there is no definition of red, for example. All people experience red for themselves, and though there is a common name for the color, we all have our own individual understanding of it.

If you have an immediate emotional response to the idea of broken bicycles rusting in the rain, the songwriter has bypassed your brain and gone straight to your soul.

It's similar to the beauty of radio dramas that feed you with images and ideas and allow you to invent pictures in your mind. A song can be an active experience in which both the listener and the writer are bringing something to a song. Many people dislike music videos because they discourage songwriters and listeners from imagining their own visions—they supply preconceived visuals.

In the songs of the great songwriters you will notice an abundant use of imagery. That is because it's always more powerful to *show* us something than to *tell* us something. Instead of writing, "I feel sad/everything is wrong/life is bad/and lasts too long," write something that makes us feel that way for ourselves. There are countless dance songs that say little besides, "I want you, I need you, oooh baby, let's dance all night." Sure, that kind of writing has its place but it's been done, there's nothing new or revealing in it. Compare that to the rich imagery and sense of time and place in Tom Waits' "Invitation to the Blues" (from *Small Change*):

And you feel just like Cagney, she looks like Rita
*   Hayworth*
At the counter of the Schwab's drugstore
You wonder if she might be single

Nowadays, too many songs don't have any *nouns* in them at all, and refer to little in the actual world. Yes, all of us have emotions but simply *stating* abstract emotions in songs is not effective. Instead, *show* something in a song, something *concrete*, that allows us to generate our own emotions. Holly Near told *SongTalk*: "People who are vague in songs are afraid of something. They're afraid to be specific." She's right. Songwriters often take the easy way out, using general language instead of realizing that they have songs in them that no other person could write. Your particular slant on life is completely individual, and the combination of images that have the most emotional resonance for you are yours and yours alone. Don't be afraid to use the details that mean the most to your life, and trust that if they resonate for you they will also resonate for others.

Another good example is Paul Simon's song "You're Kind" with this verse:

I'm gonna leave you now . . .
I like to sleep with the window open
And you keep the window closed . . .

The use of the window imagery is revealing because it works on more than one level at a time. There is the literal meaning that the man actually left because he can't sleep with closed windows. And there is the larger meaning of needing openness and rebelling against being closed in in any way. Again, Simon could have expressed this same thing in emotional terms such as "I need my freedom, you make me feel trapped." But by using a concrete image he allows the listener to see and feel the situation rather than having it told to him.

▼ *What is a metaphor?*

A metaphor, according to Webster, is a figure of speech in which one word or phrase literally denoting one kind of object or idea is used in place of another to suggest a likeness between them. "Metaphor" is both a particular figure of speech and, more generally, any kind of figurative language, such as similes, puns, and double entendre.

A simile is one way of showing a likeness between two words or ideas by using the words "like" or "as." For example, a simile would be "the sky is black as coal." A metaphor would be "the sky is coal." A metaphor for freedom, then, brings us back to our last example, an open window.

Metaphorical writing allows writers to express abstract feelings in an identifiable way. The songwriter can reach for an emotion beyond concrete language. Dylan employed a metaphorical title to sum up the feeling of reckless loneliness with these words: "How does it feel to be on your own/with no direction home. . . . like a rolling stone?"

▼ *Is it a good idea to include the truth—actual facts from your own life—in a song?*

Yes. I think that using actual facts can lend more resonance to a song. But there is the fine line between using facts from your own life to paint a larger picture and writing only about your own little world. Can you use these facts to root your song in reality while still writing a universal song, a song relatable even to people who don't know you?

Paul Simon once said that you could write a song called "My Coat" and in it you could go through all of the pockets and write about what you find there. But who would find it interesting besides you? Everyone has their own coats with their own pockets, so your job as a songwriter is to find a way that expresses that which we all share, and that which connects us.

▼ *Which is the best voice to use in a song? I like to use first person, but I hear a lot of songs in third person as well.*

It depends on the nature of the song and its requirements. The answer to this question and so many others: let the song guide you. Let it determine what is necessary for the music and the mood that you are creating.

All voices can be used effectively in a song. The use of the first person is probably the most common approach, centering the song around the voice of an "I," as in "I Want to Hold Your Hand," by the Beatles. It can be a simple, clean, and effective way of centering a song.

First person

First person can also be used when telling a story from a character's point of view, as in many of Randy Newman's songs. In this voice, you can reveal much about the narrator himself by his slant on things, what Randy refers to as the use of the "untrustworthy narrator." Newman's song "Short People," for example, is not about height; it is about the prejudice of its narrator.

Randy Newman discussed the use of this voice with *SongTalk*: "I love things where the audience knows stuff that the narrator doesn't know. I *love* that kind of stuff. You don't see it much in *songs*. You see it in literature a little bit. If someone said to me, 'What makes your songs different,' that is it. They are first person but they're not about me."

The inherent danger of this method, using the first person to make a point about the narrator herself, is that people will misinterpret the first-person voice as the songwriter's voice—or the singer's voice once the song is recorded. So you have to do your job well and provide enough clues so that the listener is alerted to the fact that a point is being made *about* the narrator rather than by the narrator. Even Newman, who is a master at this technique, has had his songs like "Short People" and "Rednecks" criticized because people took them literally and missed the point. Part of this is due to the fact that people don't always listen carefully to songs. For this reason, be certain that your meaning and intention is clear and holds up to scrutiny.

Second person

Use of the second-person voice—"you"—is also common in songs and quite valid. In this voice, the listener is brought into the song. Instead of hearing a story related that has already happened, the second person voice involves the listener directly and draws him into the song, as in Carole King's "You've Got a Friend." Similarly, Simon's "Bridge Over Troubled Water," another song of friendship and devotion, uses the second-person voice as a vow of comfort:

When you're down and out
When you're on the street
When evening falls so hard, I will comfort you.

Even songs that tell a story about a person can be told in second person *to* that person instead of about him. Don McClean's "Vincent" is a good example, a classic song about Van Gogh that encapsulates the artist's life, work, and state of mind but does it all in the second voice, directing the song to Van Gogh himself: "Starry starry night, paint your palette blue and gray/Look out on a summer's day with eyes that know the darkness in my soul . . ." The listener, though, is never excluded; we are involved not only by the magnificent melody and vivid imagery but also by the concluding commentary with which we can empathize: ". . . but I could have told you, Vincent, this world was never meant for one as beautiful as you."

Third person

Use of the third person in a song, using "he," "she," or "they" is appropriate when telling a story in narrative form. Many of Woody Guthrie's songs, such as "Tom Joad" (which he based on the movie *The Grapes of Wrath*) use this voice to great advantage: "Tom Joad got out of the old MacAlester Pen/There he got his parole/After four long years on a man killing charge/Tom Joad came a walking down the road."

No matter which voice you choose for your song, make sure you retain a consistency of voice by not shifting at some point in the song. Sometimes songwriters will unconsciously switch from "he" to "I" or "you," which can be confusing to a listener as well as amateurish sounding. (For example, the verses will be about a "he" while the chorus will suddenly be sung to a "you.") This can also tell you something about your song: is it truly about a "he"—someone outside of yourself—or is it about you? Choose the voice that comes closest to the heart of the song. Sometimes when working on a song about a character in third person, you realize the song is screaming out for first person and demands to be sung as "I" instead of "she." Listen to the song as it develops and follow where it leads you.

▼ ─────────────────────────────

Often it's easier to use the third person and write about a character divorced from yourself when you describe your own experience. It's not unlike going to a psychiatrist and detailing the problems of an imaginary friend instead of talking about yourself. It's not easy to say, "I feel this way," and it can be even harder to put into a song. As a songwriter, though, you don't want to run away from yourself and from your feelings. Face your fears in songwriting and see if you can deal with a subject head on instead of approaching it from a side-door or avoiding it altogether. If you are going to use the third person, do it to your advantage rather than using it to hide behind a character.

───────────────────────────── ▲

▼ Should I try to tell a whole story in a song?

Again, there is no single approach that is always best; each song requires a different approach and each one is capable of accomplishing various things.

A song exists in time, and to be experienced must be heard chronologically from beginning to end. Within a song, you can structure the way time is experienced many different ways. There can be a strict sense of time—a story that moves in time from one point to the next—as in the case of Woody Guthrie's "Tom Joad," which is a straight narrative. However, the song is seventeen verses long; it takes a lot of time to tell a story. As most songs have about three verses, telling a full story in a song can be difficult though not impossible.

Sometimes a song that contains a progression in time can be effective if it is tied to a theme that is timeless. In this way there can be a progression in time in the verses of the song but a chorus that exists outside of time. An example is the Beatles' "She's Leaving Home" from *Sgt. Pepper*. The song begins by placing the listener in a very specific time frame, identifying both the time and day: "Wednesday morning at five o'clock as the day begins . . ." The first verse then details the subject's morning activities in a narrative way so that there is a sense of time: "Silently closing the bedroom door/Leaving the note she hoped would say more/She goes downstairs to the kitchen clutching her handkerchief . . ." As the character steps outside and breaks free, so does the song from its sense of time to take on a larger view that is beyond time: "She (we gave her most of our lives) is leaving (sacrificed most of our lives) home (we gave her everything money could buy . . .) Bye Bye . . ." In this way the songwriter can utilize a progression of time in a song while stepping outside of that progression as well in the chorus.

This contrast of time/timelessness in songs is not unlike our experience of life itself, and songs can reflect this: going through a progression of time in our everyday lives while also standing separate from that temporal sense and viewing our lives as a whole, outside of time. When you experience your own memories, for example, you don't think back to the moment you were born and review your memories in chronological order. More likely you mix up memories from all parts and times of your life and experience them in an emotional rather than a sequential order. Similarly, your song can be structured in an emotional rather than a sequential way.

For example, in Joni Mitchell's "Amelia," Joni cuts between the story of Amelia Earhart in the past and her own life in the present: "A ghost of aviation/She was swallowed by the sky/Or by the sea, like me she had a dream to fly . . ."

Since songs don't age or change in time, there is no reason they need be bound by time. They can express, instead, a sense of eternity. "Strawberry Fields Forever" (from the Beatles' *Magical Mystery Tour*), for example, is based on a childhood memory of John Lennon's. Strawberry Fields was a Salvation Army home in Liverpool where Lennon spent many summer days in his youth. But like Joni Mitchell's "Amelia," the song is connected more by an emotional sense than a temporal one. Rather than attempt to capture its spirit through specific time-related instances, Lennon evokes a dreamlike, wistful remembrance that embraces all time, (hence the title "Strawberry Fields *Forever*") and emphasizes that which is timeless: "Let me take you down cause I'm going to Strawberry Fields, nothing is real and nothing to get hung about/Strawberry Fields forever." Songs can be like cubist paintings, able to show different perspectives at a single time.

▼ *I'm a lyricist and I have written countless songs without music. I see in the back of some magazines advertisements for companies that will "set your words to music" for a price. Is this a good idea, and if not, what should I do?*

This is not a good idea. Any organization that wants to take your money in exchange for this kind of service is the kind of place to avoid. There are countless other writers around the country who have an honest need for collaborators and who you do not need to pay to work with you. (See page 43 on collaboration.)

The primary reason that you should steer clear of these kinds of services is an aesthetic one: chances of your lyrics getting a proper musical treatment are minimal. These companies are strictly involved to make money, not to make good songs. This is something I've observed firsthand, having once been employed at a Hollywood recording studio where one of the most prominent of these companies recorded their "albums." No care is put into either the composing of the music for the words or the recording of the song. The melody they use for a set of words is basic and uninspired; usually a variation on a melody that has been used countless times before, altered only slightly to fit a new lyric.

The recording of the song is similarly haphazard and careless. The setup that I worked on was generally one woman singing and playing the piano; one guy on synth-bass, drum machine, and keyboard; and another on guitar. The songs were all recorded live to two-track (this means no overdubbing; no mixing) in their roughest form; a second take on any song was almost unheard of.

One of my duties was to fade out the song when it reached two-and-a-half minutes, regardless of where in the song that part came. And even when my fade-outs were poorly executed, bringing down the volume on one channel sooner than on the other, those fade-outs would be preserved forever on vinyl. The outcome was a shoddily made recording with no attention given to the artistic intention of the lyricist/songwriter.

Why, then, do so many people pay so much money each year for these kinds of recordings? They are essentially "vanity recordings," created so that people can say, "I've got a song that was recorded on an album in Hollywood and here it is." These companies understand well this motivation and cash in on it. And they do make a lot of money: not only do they charge the songwriter a lot of money for this opportunity, they also then charge the songwriter a bundle to buy the albums. The songwriters themselves are the only people that buy these poor excuses for records, and they often buy many copies to give them to friends and family who surely won't be able to find them in record stores.

And even if you *are* happy with a recording that results from one of these services, no one in the industry will take it seriously. If you are serious about your career, it would be much more beneficial to collaborate with a composer/songwriter. Put your money into your own career instead of into the pockets of "songsharks." There are far better ways to market and promote your own music (see the section on Publishing and The Music Business).

And remember: *anytime* anyone shows interest in your work yet wants any money from you to get the ball rolling, be careful! That is almost always a sure sign that you're getting involved with a shyster. I can still remember well my excitement, at the age of thirteen, when one of these types told me he not only loved my songs but the way I sang them! For a mere three thousand dollars (to cover recording and travel costs) he was going to whisk me off to the recording capital of the free world, Cincinnati, to record my songs. It was a disappointment but also a good lesson for me when I learned that it was my money and not my songs that this guy really wanted. Songwriters are vulnerable and make easy targets for these sharks.

2

Melody

▼ What is a melody?

The word "melody" grew out of the Greek Word "meloidia," which means music, or chanting.

For songwriters, the word "melody" refers to the tune of a song; the succession of musical notes in rhythm that together form a musical whole with a start and a finish. It is composed of intervals—the space between notes—and the duration of the notes.

The melody is the prominent musical line of a song. While there may be many voices singing harmony to a melody in a song, only the main voice, or basic line of the song, is the melody.

▼ Does every song have a melody?

No. There are many songs nowadays that are nonmelodic, such as rap songs that are essentially words chanted in rhythm, sans any melody. This is by no means a new invention: chanting words in rhythm goes back to the traditions of Africa where men and women chanted words in rhythm while working. It's a musical form that was brought to America and chanted in the fields by the slaves. This evolved into a form called the "talking blues," which is also a song that consists of words chanted in rhythm without an actual melody.

Most of the original talking blues had to do with ascending to heaven. Willie Dixon, a man often referred to as the Father of the Blues, explained

to *SongTalk* that when the slaves were chanting about going to heaven, they were actually using a code; going to heaven referred to returning to their homeland, Africa. "The blues in America came from work songs," Willie explained. "They used to not let the slaves sing, they wouldn't let them talk . . . But when they found out that the slaves could chant certain songs and work in time, the bosses decided to let them go and chant these songs. . . . Eventually the slaves found out, 'Why, hell, as long as he's letting us chant these songs, we can begin to pass messages'. . . . They were singing about going home: 'If I never see you no more, I'll meet you on the other shore . . . ' "

This is the essence of the folk process in which people take a form of music and adapt it to their own needs. As Pete Seeger told *SongTalk*: "The folk process is very, very strong in Africa. When African people found themselves here (in America), they just kept doing what they had been doing for centuries . . ."

Seeger and others, like Woody Guthrie, adapted the talking blues to their own needs, taking a traditional folk chant about going to heaven ("If you wanna get to heaven let me tell you what to do/gotta grease your feet in a little mutton stew . . .") and using it to discuss the need for unionization in a song like "Talking Union": "If you want higher wages let me tell you what to do/got to talk to the workers in the shop with you . . ."

Bob Dylan, who began his career imitating Woody Guthrie, wrote many talking blues, including "Talking New York." And today with rap songs, the talking blues has returned again in abundance, and with some heavy rhythm.

▼ How do I come up with melodies for songs?

There are may different approaches to the creation of melodies. Some are methods in which pure melodies are sought after; other methods include matching the right melody to a phrase or set of lines. The latter method points to the difference between creating melodies for songs as opposed to an instrumental work. In a song, a strong melody is dependent upon the lyrics to carry it; if it doesn't fit the lyrics well, no matter how powerful or fresh the melody might be, it won't be effective.

Talent does play a big part here, as some people are simply more melodically gifted than others. These people will have the easiest time thinking of melodies; they're the kind of writers for whom tunes seem to "pop into their heads." Other writers have no such serendipity and claim to work hard for every note they write. If you are in this camp, writing a good melody will be a means of trial and error, requiring lots of experimentation and a good deal of patience.

▼ Can I compose a melody without using an instrument?

Yes. There are some composers who are gifted at coming up with melodies in their head, away from an instrument. Some say that this is the best method for generating melodies because the direction of the tune is determined by the tune itself and not by the chords you play on an instrument.

Jay Livingston, the musical half of the team Livingston & Evans (who wrote "Que Será Será," "Silver Bells," and "Buttons and Bows," among other classics) told us, "I often come up with melodies in my head. I find that when you're at the piano, your hands follow old familiar patterns. If you're walking around away from the piano, you're freer. Your mind goes anywhere you want. I've written some better melodies that way." He went on to relate two stories of writing melodies in his car on the way to work. Both songs have since become standards, written in transit on Sunset Bou-

levard: "To Each His Own" and "Mona Lisa."

Melody and lyrics

Are you generating a melody based on existing lyrics or is this a melody for which words will be written later? If you are writing to an existing lyric, at least you have some structure in which you can work. An existing lyric—if written well—will provide you with the subject matter, the meter, the length of the lines, the verse-chorus pattern, etc. (More on this in song structure, page 40.) Basing a melody on an already established foundation such as this is much simpler than composing a melody apart from any lyrics—and then attempting to write words to it, or handing it over to a lyricist.

If you are writing the melody first (without a lyric pattern), be sure that it fits a regular structure. Unless you or your lyricist is an absolute genius at adapting words to music, it's tough to write a lyric to a piece of music that has an irregular structure.

Songs must be structured in a way that clearly defines the verse, chorus, or bridge sections; a song that has long melodic lines with no repeats just does not work. If you examine most songs you will see that they are based on repeating patterns. A verse melody can repeat up to six times or more in a song; a chorus, too, can repeat numerous times. A melody writer must be conscious of creating these patterns when writing a tune if that tune is to be effectively turned into a song.

Keep in mind that all listeners to songs are conditioned, having heard songs written in conventional song structures their whole lives. So they expect to hear a clearly delineated verse and chorus; they expect to have a repeating chorus that they can quickly learn themselves.

Of course, many great lyrics *have* been written to long, irregular, and complex melodies. Joni Mitchell's phenomenal lyrics to Charles Mingus' melodies on her *Mingus* album are a good example of this: colorful lyrics every bit as rich and imaginative as the music to which they match. Joni Mitchell, though, is one of the world's most gifted lyricists, and few others can approach her prowess with wedding language and melody. If you are a composer who does not write lyrics, you do not want to make the job of setting your tune to lyrics a difficult one. Even if your melody is a complex one, it will make your lyricist's job an easier one if it fits a regular structure.

Melody and harmony

Though words and music make up a song, the composer also has to determine the harmony of a song, the chord changes you choose to harmonize your melody. If you compose a melody without an instrument, it can be hard to determine the harmony unless the changes are quite basic, such as a blues progression. But if you want to use more complex chord changes, it makes sense to work on an instrument.

Plagiarism

Another thing to be conscious of when working on melodies, especially when generating them apart from an instrument, is the possibility of plagiarism. Perhaps more than in any other art form, it's quite easy to plagiarize music. The reason is obvious: when striving to write a new melody you lean toward that which moves you emotionally. And since your brain has stored up literally thousands of melodies that have moved you in the past, it's easy to land on a variation of one of them and think that it is new.

This has even happened to great songwriters who weren't trying to steal a melody but did so accidentally. The most famous example is the closeness between George Harrison's "My Sweet Lord" and "You're So Fine." Surely Harrison wouldn't have "stolen" the melody. But in writing what moved him when caught up in the rush of the creative flow, which also generated the beautiful and spiritual lyrics of the song, his mind found a melody that moved him in his youth.

Because the potential of plagiarism is so great, songwriters must train themselves to recognize an unoriginal melody as soon as they come up with one. If you suddenly find yourself with a gorgeous tune, one of those melodies that seemed to write itself, play it for yourself and make sure it doesn't belong to another song. As time goes by, this is a talent that you can improve on, and you'll find yourself telling fellow songwriters, "Yeah, it is a nice melody, too bad Gershwin already wrote it," or whoever the real writer is.

When I first started writing I was fooling around in F major trying to come up with some words about freedom. (I was young and enjoyed these big subjects.) Suddenly I came up with what seemed to me to be the most beautiful tune ever written, and I was overwhelmed by my ability to have written it. I proudly played it for my brother who immediately informed me that I had stolen the melody to "I'm a Believer," which was a hit for the Monkees at the time, written by Neil Diamond.

He was right. It was almost an identical melody to "I'm a Believer" and because I was playing it slowly and in a folky rhythm, I didn't notice. After that time, maybe simply to save myself from similar embarrassment, I became more adept at recognizing when I've ripped off somebody else's tune.

But being a crafty songwriter and one who never throws anything away on purpose, I kept that song and simply changed around the tune to the point where it no longer resembled Neil Diamond or the Monkees. And this is a good tip: if you find that your song is too close to another, don't discard it. (As Jackson Browne once said, "All unfinished songs are like pieces of wood out of which someday a beautiful guitar can be built.") Take your melody and change it around. Change the pattern of the notes, the places where it rises and falls. Enlarge the range of the melody if you can, adding new notes where the melody returns to the same note. Switch the chord changes. Try it in a different rhythm. Allow these changes to inspire and encourage you to write an even better melody than what you started with. Do whatever it takes to change the melody and make it your own.

After all, there are only so many possible usages of the notes in the scale; every song is somewhat of a variation on another, and these variations extend the ever-growing branches of music while sharing the same roots. And even if your song is sparked by someone else's song, after you have filtered it through your individual sensibilities, it will be your own. Even the greats have been "inspired" by other writers' songs to create a great one of their own: Paul McCartney admitted that he wrote "Let It Be" under the influence of Paul Simon's "Bridge Over Troubled Water," yet the two songs sound nothing alike. Becker and Fagen of

Steely Dan, two of pop music's most original songwriters, conceded that the saxophone riff that is the basis for their song "Gaucho" was "heavily influenced" by Keith Jarrett's "Belonging." In fact, the resemblance between the two melodies is extremely close, but Becker and Fagen use the tune in an entirely new and inventive way and make it their own.

Lamont Dozier said, "Every note has been played. Every beat has been beat, so to speak. I might come up with something different but music is not something I invented. It was here long before any of us were here. So if you're serious about having a career, listen to everything. Writing is a personal thing but you do have influences. . . . It all starts with the heart, with writing what moves you."

▼ How do you write melodies using an instrument?

You can think of the melody line by itself or you can think of it in relation to the harmony. To work on a melody apart from the harmony (not thinking of the chord changes), a piano or keyboard is an easier instrument to use than a guitar because of its layout: the notes are set up in front of you in order. If you play your melody, you can try out variations and note choices on the piano that you might not think of without an instrument. Instead of your having to depend on the prowess of your own singing voice, the piano can do the work for you.

Another way to generate melodies is by experimenting with the harmony—the chord changes—to see what melodic ideas you might imagine. Simply play one chord either on a piano/keyboard or on a guitar—a C-major chord, for example—and see if it leads you anywhere. Play the chord in a simple rhythm and try singing any tune to it. Notice that you can start the melody on many different notes and it will still match the C-major chord.

Then, if you are adventurous, try combining it with another chord, say, an A-minor chord. Play the C first for a few beats and then switch to the A minor, and see what, if any, melodic ideas arrive. Many songs have been written using only those two chords! Notice the great richness of melody you can create with only those two chords. As time

goes on and you work with chords often, you will become familiar with chord relationships.

▼ Are there any dangers in using chord changes to generate melodies?

Yes. The danger lies in letting yourself get too restricted by the chords you are playing. Melodically it's important to remember that beauty lies not only in how a melody works with a chord, but also in how it works *against* a chord.

An A-minor chord, for example, consists of three notes: A, C, and E. When playing the chord to come up with melody ideas, the use of those three notes is most obvious. To use another note, however, you don't have to move to another chord. The use of a note not in the chord will create a certain dissonance, and dissonance creates tension. And the beauty of all melodies lies not in their static nature but in the process of tension and release. So be aware when writing melodies to chord changes of the notes that work against as well as with chords.

A good example is the song "Same Girl" from Randy Newman's *Trouble in Paradise* album. The melody on the opening phrase is played against an A-minor chord that goes with these words: "You're still the same girl . . ." The notes in that phrase are, in order: E, A, B, C, A. And all of those notes, with the exception of the B, are in the A-minor chord. It is that B, the note falling on the word "the," that works against the chord, providing a beautiful dissonance that Randy doesn't race over; he stays on it as long as the other notes. In the key of A minor, the B is the minor second. And the minor second is a notoriously beautiful interval. Not only is it pleasing to the ear, it provides that tension which releases with the arrival of the next note, the C, that the B leads us to.

When working on melodies based on chord changes, experiment with notes that aren't in the basic triad, and in this way your melodies will become more expressive. It doesn't have to be a minor chord, either. Try the interval of a major second played against a major chord—a D against a C-major chord, for example, and check out the results!

Writing any kind of music depends on a good deal of listening to the music and where it wants to go. Rather than force the melody into a direction, listen to it and try to follow it. Often a melody can tell you where to go and what chord to use. In the beginning of Charlie Chaplin's "Smile," the melody begins on an F-major chord and stays within the framework of that chord. (See exam-

SMILE, tho' your heart is ach – ing,   SMILE, e – ven tho' it's break–ing,

ple.) The melody begins on an F, slopes upward to the third, A, and gently downwards to the D on the line "Smile, tho' your heart is aching." At this point the melody could have returned to the F again, starting the next phrase on the same word and the same note. But instead, the melody slips down below the F to an E natural, adding a beautiful sense of sadness against the F-major chord beginning the phrase, "Smile, even tho' it's breaking." The melody changes the direction of the chord; the effect is that of an F-major seventh chord (as E natural is a major seventh above F). This chord is slightly dissonant and creates a feeling of tension that needs to be resolved; it leads down to the solid fifth, the C natural, to resolve the chord.

Tension and release

The thing that distinguishes an okay melody from a strong one is often the use of tension and release. To make your chorus sound especially explosive, you can create tension and the need for resolution in the verse to be resolved in the chorus.

An example of this is "You've Lost That Lovin' Feelin'" by Barry Mann, Cynthia Weil, and Phil Spector. The song is in the key of C and yet the very first chord creates tension: a B flat with C in the bass (B flat/C). The chord hangs underneath the C major, and pulls us up toward it. It's used for two measures, resolves to the C major, and then repeats the process: tension is created and resolved twice before we even get to the first chorus. The momentum is then increased by a series of ascending chords that lead us up the scale to the dominant: Dm7, Em7, F maj 7, F/G, and finally G. The G is the dominant or V chord in the key of C, and it propels us back to the tonic chord, the C major.

That chord comes after this huge build-up, this creation of tension, and resolves with the chorus on the title line: "You've lost that lovin' feelin'." The effect is a build-up that increases in intensity until it explodes on the chorus and then repeats the process after the chorus with the next verse.

None of this build-up of tensions would be worthwhile, of course, if the payoff wasn't great. The chorus of "You've Lost That Lovin' Feelin'" is sufficiently powerful to stand up to that kind of build-up. A big build-up to a disappointing chorus only intensifies that sense of dissatisfaction; make sure your resolution is not a letdown.

▼ Which instrument is best for writing music, piano or guitar?

There is no definitive answer. Whichever instrument you are most proficient at is the best one for you. Each has both positive attributes and negative qualities.

The piano has something the guitar does not—the keyboard—which beautifully lays out every note from the first to the last in order before your eyes. This enables a composer to see a melody and the way it works against chord sequences, something that is not as clear on guitar. Also, because of the piano's layout, it is easy to play a melody and an accompaniment at the same time, which is not easy to do on guitar.

Some composers have suggested that a piano is better for coming up with interesting and unusual chords for another reason. When you play a plain C-major chord on a guitar it can sound rich and resonant. On a piano it seems rather simple and pedestrian. This encourages the piano-playing composer to alter that chord in imaginative ways, something that is easier to do on a piano than a guitar. While on guitar it can be difficult to play a chord change against a repeating pedal tone in the bass, it's easy on piano. Songs written on a piano, as opposed to guitar songs, are usually more harmonically complex. Songs by piano-based composers, such as Burt Bacharach and Jimmy Webb, are much more richly complex harmonically than songs written on guitar.

Other composers say that there's no truth to that idea. "A C-major chord on a Steinway grand sounds pretty damn grand," one of them said. "Better than a guitar ever sounds."

The guitar, because of its makeup, encourages rhythmic playing of chords; it is set up to form chords with the left hand while strumming with the right hand, providing a rhythm. And because it is more portable than a piano, it is easy to write rhythmic songs on a guitar and still have a freedom of movement you can't have while tied to the piano.

For this reason, rock songs and R&B songs are well suited for the guitar. Carole King, who has written countless classics on piano, recently started playing guitar for a new approach to composition, resulting in rockier songs. As she told *SongTalk*, "It [the guitar] is the portable axe! I've moved to electric guitar recently and now I really get down and rock. It's given me a new dimension, a new place to go."

Using both piano (or another keyboard instrument) and guitar seems to be the most effective method. While many composers have never played both, if you can switch back and forth you have more tools at hand. If you have been writing a song on piano and you need a more rhythmic chorus, you might want to switch to guitar to work on the chorus. Or if you've finished a song on guitar that could stand improvement, you can play it on the piano, hear it in that setting, and see if that leads you to any new ideas about the song. My experience is that a song written on the guitar that is then played on piano will sound quite different; the strengths or weaknesses of the chord sequence, especially, and its relation to the melody line will be emphasized.

Even if you are much more proficient on one instrument than the other, it is still beneficial to switch back and forth. Many guitarists have what James Taylor called the "claw approach" to piano playing, essentially a form of strumming chords on a piano. Even if this is the best you can do, the nature of the instrument will likely lead you into new directions that the guitar did not suggest.

▼ Do I need a tape recorder for songwriting?

For a composer, a tape recorder can be extremely helpful. While a few of us can notate music with as much alacrity as a Mozart, any of us can sing a tune into a tape recorder and preserve it instantly. This is a great tool, one that previous generations of songwriters have not had.

▼ ─────────────────────────

When the printing press was first invented, many feared that it was harmful. The reasoning was that people would not remember anything if they could store their memories in books. Similarly, some composers feel that relying on a tape recorder will be detrimental to their ability to recall melody. I feel that the tape recorder is about as harmful as the book has proved to be; it is a tool that makes the job easier and allows us to put our energies into the solving of harder problems.

───────────────────────── ▲

Whether at an instrument or away from one, having a recorder handy makes a lot of sense. Often you will come up with melodies spontaneously—in the car even or at your desk at work. If you have a recorder nearby, you can quickly save that tune and work on it later.

This is also beneficial for lyricists, who might come up with lyric ideas at strange times and need to store them. The new minicassettes on the market are both inexpensive and very useful. Small enough to keep in a jacket pocket, and simple enough to operate with one hand, they are perfect for picking up while driving—or in the midst of some other activity—and using immediately. They are also nice because more elaborate setups, especially where you need to set up mikes or thread tapes, can interrupt the spontaneity of the creative flow. These minicassettes are so small that they don't draw attention to themselves; they sit quietly while recording adequately whatever you need.

Sometimes certain melodies are so special that they will stay in your mind no matter what; you won't be able to forget them, a pretty good sign that this is a powerful tune. Melodies that are easy to forget might be that way precisely because they are forgettable. As Jazz legend Mose Allison said,

"If I can't remember a song, I figure it wasn't worth remembering."

▼ Is a drum machine a good tool to use while writing songs?

A drum machine can provide a steady rhythm that might inspire you to come up with musical ideas. Many songwriters like using drum machines; others feel that they provide a stiff, emotionless structure that is more restrictive than helpful for writing. Some writers enjoy the constant rhythmic foundation that a drum machine can provide and are able to write very human songs based on the mechanic support of a machine. Bruce Hornsby, for example, whose songs are quite emotional, often uses drum machines to get him going; even a beautiful song such as "The Way It Is" was born on the beat of a machine.

It makes sense to determine what kind of song you are writing. If you are working on a dance tune, a funk tune, or an R&B number, a drum machine can be beneficial in getting a good groove established.

If your song is a ballad or otherwise based more on melody than rhythm, the drum machine could get in the way. Determine what your needs are and don't always depend on the machine.

▼ ───────────────────

Some writers dislike drum machines because their tempos are always perfect like a metronome and they never speed up the way a human drummer usually does, thus lacking any human passion or emotion. At the same time, playing parts to a drum machine rhythm is excellent for any musician as it helps to get your own sense of tempo more constant. This will enable a musician to be more professional in a studio situation when it comes time to overdub parts. If you are playing a keyboard part, for example, to an existing part, your time, or sense of tempo, has to be very strict to match the track. And playing with a drum machine is wonderful practice, just as playing to a metronome is good for perfecting your sense of time.

───────────────── ▲

▼ How do I use a drum machine when writing?

A drum machine plays rhythmic patterns that are one measure long. It can repeat one pattern over and over again or it can be programmed to play many patterns in a certain order. (In drum machine language, this is the difference between "writing a pattern" and "writing a song.")

When working on a song, one pattern is often enough to establish a foundation of rhythm. (This is not to imply that a single pattern is sufficient for the rhythm of an entire song. It can be sufficient, though, as a basis for the formation of your first musical ideas.) When a song is complete and you want to record a demo, you can then program the machine to play different patterns in the order of the finished song, thus creating a full drum track for your piece.

Peter Gabriel's beautiful "Mercy Street" (from *So*) was based on a simple repeating pattern played on triangles. From that humble start a beautiful song was created. Similarly, his hit "Sledgehammer" from the same album, a jubilant, upbeat song, was based on a very basic drum machine pattern. As his producer, Daniel Lanois, explained, the great sense of rhythm was created on the guitars. Often rhythm is based not only on the sound of a drum pattern, but on the *interaction* of other instruments, such as bass, guitar, and keyboards, with the drums. It's the way that all the pieces fit together that makes a rhythm work.

John Lennon once said that all you need is a solid backbeat to make a rock song sound right. And while there are innumerable rhythmic patterns a songwriter can use, the backbeat is the most common pattern to use in pop or rock (for a song in 4/4 or 2/4 time).

A backbeat emphasizes the second and fourth beat of each measure, and it is commonly played on the snare drum (the snare being either on a drum machine or a real set of drums). It is a backbeat (as opposed to the downbeat) that is the first beat of each measure.

To set up a backbeat pattern, you establish the downbeat first. To do this you need a count of four, which you can establish with a high hat playing on each beat: one, two, three, and four. Once your count of four is established, adjust the tempo until it is approximately right for the kind of song you want to write. Then add a bass drum on beats one and three to establish the downbeat. Set the snare drum to play on the backbeat—beats two and four. And the result will be a basic backbeat pattern, about the most basic you can get. As you become familiar with it, you can play with the placement of the bass drum, using it to accent as well as provide the downbeat. And after that point, understanding the basics of creating a single rhythmic pattern, you can create more diverse patterns—with or without a backbeat—and string them together to form full songs.

Each drum machine is a little different to program, so I won't attempt to delve into the technicalities of programming. Use the instructions for your particular machine and the help of friends to get you accustomed to the basics of programming patterns into your unit. Once you know how to program and hear rhythms, you can set up a backbeat pattern or any other rhythmic pattern to use as the foundation for a song.

You can create an unusual pattern, one you haven't tried before, to move you in a rhythmic direction that you might not ordinarily follow. It's easy to get trapped into the routine of always writing songs to the same rhythm, and a drum machine can be effective in forcing you to try new things.

Peter Gabriel used a drum machine not to set up predictable patterns, but to invent fresh, unusual tapestries of rhythm that he would then teach to a drummer. The drum machine is a fine tool for this process. While it is often difficult to write down unusual rhythms and even harder to relate them with words, on a drum machine you can capture and alter rhythms easily and then preserve them for later use.

If you are the type of writer for whom writing to a drum machine is constricting, overly time-consuming, or simply unexciting, don't bother then. You might want to have one to use in the demo process and never in the writing process. Do what feels best for you and remember that it is the song that ultimately matters. An unusual rhythm pattern is useless if it isn't part of a well-written song. Don't fall into the trap of thinking that production can make a song work. Production can enrich a song, but only the right combination of words and music can make a great song.

▼ *When I come up with a good melody, how should I save it?*

There are three ways. The first is to play the melody over so many times to yourself that it gets instilled in your head. This is a dangerous method as you may easily forget the melody later even if you think you've learned it. The reason is that a mind cannot think of more than one melody at a time. As you know if you've ever been writing a song when someone turns on some music, it's next to impossible to play one tune with another one going. Even if you've taught yourself a melody, hearing another one can quickly jumble up that memory.

Another problem with this method is that the freshest melodies created usually are fresh precisely because they are different than others you have written. Perhaps they take an unusual turn or make an unexpected skip that you've rarely made before. As you attempt to remember it by repetition, you might find yourself moving toward a more normal melody and losing whatever it was that made the new one sound new.

So you've got to preserve it in other ways. There are two other methods: You can tape it or notate it. To tape it, try getting a small compact tape machine. The new minicassettes on the market—the kind that many business people use for dictation—are ideal because they are tiny, run on batteries, and are easy to use in a flash. If you have more complex equipment that requires plugging in mikes or patching in cords or anything like that, you can get distracted before saving your melody. You need something you can get to immediately before the melody starts to fade or change.

Often the best things you come up with are happy accidents. As you may never again be able to duplicate these bursts of sudden inspiration, if you've got a tape recorder handy that you can turn on and use immediately, that will make the entire process of preserving melodies easier for you.

The third method is notation: writing down the notes in music transcription. If you are adept at this (and it requires, of course, a knowledge of music theory and ear training), then this might be the best method for you. If you do it enough, you can eventually write down notes without an instrument, and this can be very handy if you are nowhere near an instrument or a tape recorder.

However, if you are slow at figuring out the notes to your song or melody, get a tape recorder. A song can always be transcribed at a later date, but if you forget the melody it will be gone forever.

▼ *One of the things I sometimes have trouble with when writing melodies is ending phrases. How can I end phrases without sounding predictable?*

This is a common problem. When you're in a major key, the obvious way to end a final cadence is to return to the tonic, or the root chord. This resolves whatever tension might have been created in the verse. Even if the tension is not great, but is merely a dominant, or V chord, the most natural resolution would be to tonic. This has been used for thousands of years, explaining why it sounds predictable. Sometimes the tendency to return to tonic can be used to your advantage as it gives a phrase great finality and resolution. But if the song calls for something else, something more unusual, then you have to go elsewhere. This brings us to a discussion of basic music theory, so that all of these terms will be understandable. If you already know these fundamentals of music, congratulations! Skip ahead to the next chapter. If not, stay tuned.

3

Music Theory

▼ What is a scale?

A scale is a progression of notes within one octave moving from the low end to the high end. In western music the two most common scales are the major and minor scale. But there are others, such as the blues scale that is the basis for virtually every blues song.

▼ What is an octave?

An octave is the series of eight notes that make up a major or minor scale; it comes from the Latin word for the number eight, "octavus." In an octave, the first and eight notes are the same, as in: do, re, mi, fa, so, la, ti, do. Both "dos" are the same note, but they are an octave apart. Thus, if two people sing in "octaves," it means that they are singing the same note but in different registers, one octave apart.

More commonly, then, the word octave is also used to refer to the interval between two notes that are an octave apart. From a low D to the next D up, for example, is an octave. (See example. More on intervals later.)

▼ What are sharps and flats?

They are the accidentals, which means the signs used to raise or lower a natural pitch one half step.

The sharp sign is #, and when added to a note makes it one half step *higher*. A C sharp is one half step higher than C.

The flat sign is flat, and when added to a note makes the note one half step *lower*. A B flat is one half step lower than a B natural.

The flats and sharps are the black keys on the piano, and the natural notes are the white keys (with the exception of a C flat which is actually the same as a B natural, a white key; and E sharp, which is the same as F, another white key).

There's also a symbol to indicate when a note is natural and not a sharp or flat. This is the natural symbol (natural). It is used when a note has already been designated as sharp or flat, and the composer wants it to be natural (without a sharp or flat).

The terms "sharp" and "flat" are also used to describe if a tone, either sung or played, is too high or too low. If someone is singing flat, for example, he is singing some of the notes lower than they should be sung. Similarly, if a singer is sharp, it means that he is hitting the notes too high. If a guitar is out of tune, it means that its strings are sharp or flat.

▼ What's a major scale?

A major scale is the most common scale to Western ears: it is the scale used when we sing "do, re, mi, fa, so, la, ti, do." (Those syllables originate in the French solfège.) If you sing this phrase with "do" beginning on C, you are singing a C-major scale. Likewise, you can sing a major scale by beginning it on any of the twelve tones we recognize in Western Music. Each major scale is based on the combination of whole steps and half steps. A half step is distance between two consecutive notes on the piano; it is the smallest interval a piano can play. (In other words, a quarter step does exist, but to play one on a piano you'd have to play between the keys.) The distance between a C and a C sharp is a half step. Two half steps make up a whole step, so that the distance between C and D is a whole step since it is made up of two half steps: C to C sharp and C sharp to D.

To play a C-major scale on the piano, you play all white notes from C to C. But you will notice that while there are black keys between almost all of the white notes, there are no black keys between E and F and between B and C. Both of these intervals—from E to F and from B to C—are half steps. Every other interval that makes up the C-major scale is a whole step. In this way, we can see how every major scale is constructed, as the same patterns of intervals that make up a C-major scale also make up every other major scale.

Every major scale is made up of this pattern:

Whole step, whole step, half step, whole step, whole step, whole step, half step.

To simplify, I'll substitute W for whole step and H for half step, so that the pattern for a major scale is this:

W, W, H, W, W, W, H.

In musical transcription, this looks like this:

By using this pattern, you can build a major scale starting on any of the twelve tones. Let's try one starting on D.

The first note is the tonic:

D

then a whole step to:

E

another whole step would not go to F natural, which is a half step, but to:

F#

Then a half step to:

G

a whole step to:

A

another whole step to:

B

another whole step, not to C natural, a half step, but to

C#

and the final half step, which bring us back to "do":

D

The scale of D major, then, is:

D E F# G A B C# D

or:

You will notice that to make the pattern work, two notes had to be sharped, F sharp and C sharp. Hence, the key of D is a key that has two sharps. Every major key has a certain number of sharps or flats, except for the key of C major, which has none.

▼ ──────────────────────────

Solfège is the French word for a kind of ear-training and sight-singing exercise in which one sings written music using the syllables of the "solmization" system, which are: do, re, mi, fa, so, la, ti, do.

But where did these notes come from? Did they first originate in the song from *The Sound of Music*? No, of course not. They were invented to be used instead of the letter names for the notes by Guido D'Arezzo, who used them to teach students how to read music.

There are two ways that the system works.

The first is the "movable do" system in which "do" always stands for the tonic. In the key of C, C is do; in A, A is do, etc.

The other is the "fixed do" system in which do always stands for C, re always stands for D, etc. The key of D, for example, would be: re, me, fa, so, la, ti, do, re.

──────────────────────────────────▲

▼ What is a minor scale?

A minor scale is not smaller in any way than a major scale—it has the same number of notes—nor it is less important. It used to be called an Aeolian scale, meaning that it is a scale built on the sixth, rather than the tonic. To hear what this sounds like, go to the piano and in the key of C major play all the notes from A (the sixth note in the key of C) to A. Since we're in C, all of the notes are on the white keys:

A B C D E F G A

You'll see that you no longer have the familiar "do-re-mi" melody of the major scale. Instead, you have a tune that, in comparison, is kind of melancholy. This is an A-minor scale; the key of A minor, like the key of C major, has no sharps or flats. It shares the same key signature and is therefore related to the key of C. Thus, A minor is the "relative minor" to the key of C major. And it works both ways: C major is the "relative major" to the key of A minor. Every minor key has a relative major and every major key as a relative minor.

One difference between minor and major scales is that while there is only one kind of major scale, there are actually three kinds of minor scales. There is the "modal minor" (also known as the natural minor), the "melodic minor," and the "harmonic minor."

The principle sound that determines all three kinds of minor scales is the flatted third. And the only real way to understand the effect of a flatted third is to hear one. Go to a piano, or another instrument if a piano or keyboard is not available. Starting on C, play three notes in succession: C, D, E. This is a sound you're used to, "do-re-mi." Now, play the same two first notes, C and D, but play an E flat instead of the E natural. Do you hear how

vast the difference is between the two? It is that sound—the flatted third—that is at the heart of all minor scales and minor chords.

This flatted third at the beginning of the scale is the same in every kind of minor key. The difference between the different kinds of minor scales lies in the way that they end.

The A-minor scale we have already spelled out is the first kind of minor scale, the modal or natural minor. It is the purest minor scale, which is built on the following pattern of whole tones and half tones:

A B C D E F G A

W H W W H W W

The modal minor ends with a whole step—in the key of A minor, it is the whole step from G to A. However, when singers performed a piece of music in the modal minor that contained a movement from that A down a whole step to the G and back again, they found themselves changing it and singing a half step instead, as it sounded more natural. So instead of moving from A to G to A, they sang instead: A, G sharp, A. This placed a half step at the end of the minor scale instead of a whole step, and this new scale was called a "harmonic minor." Having a half step there between the seventh and eighth notes of the scale means that the interval between the sixth and seventh notes of the scale is now larger: a step and a half, also known as an "augmented second." The reason this occurs is that when we moved before the sixth note, F, to the seventh note, G, it was a whole step. Now that we have made the G into a G sharp, the interval from the F to the G sharp is bigger than a whole step; it's an "augmented second."

Therefore, the pattern for the harmonic minor is the same as the modal minor until it gets to that sixth note:

Harmonic minor:

A B C D E F G#   A

W H W W H aug.2nd H

Play this pattern on the piano and you will recognize the peculiar nature of the harmonic minor scale, which centers around that augmented second and the half step at the end of the scale. While this is no problem to play on the piano, singing that augmented second can be difficult (although very pretty, especially to modern ears). So another kind of minor scale evolved, and that is the "melodic minor" scale.

The "melodic minor" scale is a scale that changes depending on which direction it is going in. When *ascending* the scale, the final half step from the harmonic minor scale was retained, but to avoid singing that weird interval of the augmented second, the sixth note of the scale was also raised. However, when *descending* this scale, there seemed to be no need for that final half step and so a normal modal minor scale was used, which raised neither the sixth nor seventh notes of the scale.

Therefore, the pattern for the melodic minor when it is *ascending* is:

A B C D E F# G# A

W H W W W   W   H

and when it is *descending* it's the same as the modal minor:

A G F E D C B A

W W H W W H W

▼ *What is meant by tonic?*

In music, the *tonic* is the root note, or the first note, of a scale. In a C-major scale, C is tonic. In a D-major scale, D is tonic.

Tonic is also referred to as the keynote of a scale. And tonic applies both to major and minor keys. In a C-minor scale, for example, C is the tonic.

▼ *What is meant by terms like "dominant," "subdominant," etc?*

Each one of the eight notes of a major or minor scale has a different name. As we've already mentioned, the word "tonic" refers to the first note of a scale. The rest of the names are as follows:

- *I* (**do**) Tonic.
- *II* (**re**) Supertonic (one note above the tonic).
- *III* (**mi**) Mediant (halfway between the tonic and the dominant).
- *IV* (**fa**) Subdominant (below the dominant).
- *V* (**so**) Dominant (so called because of its powerful role in music, second in importance only to tonic).
- *VI* (**la**) Submediant (midway between the tonic and the subdominant).
- *VII* (**ti**) Leading note (one note below the tonic. It's the note that leads up to the tonic).
- *I* (**do**) Tonic.

▼ *What is a key, as in "This song is in the key of C"?*

A key is a group of tones that are all related to the same tonal center, or tonic. The key of C is a group of tones that revolve around the root note of C natural. The key establishes a sense of tonality; in the key of C major, the tonality revolves around the use of the C as tonic.

▼ *What is a key signature?*

The key signature is the pattern of sharps or flats placed at the beginning of all sheet music (after the clef and before the time signature). As each key has its own predetermined number of sharps or flats (or none, as in the case of C major and A minor), the key signature lets you know which key the composition is in.

For example, we've already seen that the key of D has two sharps: F sharp and C sharp. We learned this when we constructed a major scale from D to D. A good exercise that will enable you to see firsthand how many sharps or flats are in a key is to construct a major scale, using the pattern we spelled out above, on every note there is. But if you appreciate the fact that this isn't school and you're not obliged to figure out things on your own, I'll do the work for you.

It's helpful to keep in mind that many notes have two different names depending on how you look at them. On a piano, a G sharp and an A flat are the same thing. Whether you use a sharp or a flat to name the note depends on if you are in a sharp or a flat key. In a flat key, for example, you might have a C flat instead of a B, although they are the same note.

Here are the number of sharps and flats in each major key and in each major key's relative minor key:

SHARP KEYS:

Major Key	Sharps	Relative Minor Key
G	1	E minor
D	2	B minor
A	3	F# minor
E	4	C# minor
B	5	G# minor
F#	6	D# minor
C#	7	A# minor

FLAT KEYS:

Major Key	Flats	Relative Minor Key
F	1	D minor
B flat	2	G minor
E flat	3	C minor
A flat	4	F minor
D flat	5	B flat minor
G flat	6	E flat minor
C flat	7	A flat minor

▼ What is a key change?

In a song, a key change is a place where the song moves from one key into another. This is also known as "modulation." To modulate, musically, means to move from one key to another. In songs, this movement is usually an ascending one, adding intensity to a chorus, for example, by changing keys and singing it in a key that is up a step. Sometimes key changes, if they are not subtle, can sound extremely corny. However, if done with some subtlety, a key change can add extra power to a song without being overly dramatic.

A good example of a subtle key change is the final verse of Paul Simon's "Still Crazy After All These Years," which is in the key of G and moves, almost imperceptibly, to the key of A. It happens in this verse at the bottom of this page.

The modulation occurs not at the beginning of a section, as in most key changes, but in the middle of a section, right before the beginning of the line "but I would not be convicted . . ." The modulation gives the verse an added and unexpected lift, one that is almost subliminal: you might not notice it consciously but you feel it and respond to it.

▼ If a key change is also called a modulation, what is meant by the word "mutation" when it is used musically?

A key change that moves from a major key to a minor key starting on the same note (say, from A major to A minor, or from G sharp major to G sharp minor) is a "mutation."

▼ What is meant by terms like "a second, a third, a fourth," etc.?

Each degree of the scale is a different interval from the tonic. Let's look at our C-major scale again: **C D E F G A B C**

Quite simply, C is the first note and is called the tonic. D is the second note of the scale, so it is called the second. E is the third, F is the fourth, G is the fifth, A is the sixth, and B is the seventh.

The interval from C to D, then, is the interval of a second. The interval from C to E is a third. The interval from C to F is a fourth, and so on.

Octaves, fourths, and fifths are called perfect intervals—from C to F is a perfect fourth. The other intervals based on a major scale are called major intervals—from C to D is a major second and from C to E is a major third. If you lower these major intervals a half step, they are called minor intervals—from C to E flat is a minor third (remember the minor or flatted third is the one thing all minor scales have in common). There are also augmented and diminished intervals. Earlier we saw that an augmented second occurs in the harmonic minor scale (see p. 25.) An augmented second is one half step bigger than a major second. Any major or perfect interval raised a half step becomes an augmented interval. Any perfect interval lowered a half step is called diminished. From C to G is a perfect fifth; from C to G flat is a diminished fifth (also called a flatted fifth for obvious reasons).

▼ What is dissonance?

Dissonance occurs when two or more notes clash in a way that is jarring to our ears. A chord that has a dissonant interval in it is a dissonant chord and can be said to possess "discord" as opposed to "concord."

The opposite of dissonance is "consonance," which refers to intervals or chords that are not jarring but are pleasant to the ears. (Knowing the roots of words often helps to understand them. "Dissonance" comes from two Latin words: "dissonare" that means "to be discordant," and "sonus" that means "sound" or "melody." Dissonance, then, is a discordant sound.)

Dissonance creates tension, which creates a need to resolve toward consonance. To end a song or a phrase, then, we almost always end on a consonant chord or interval to give the feeling of finality.

But what makes some intervals dissonant and others not? The answer is our ears. As the centuries

have progressed and composers have used more adventurous chords and intervals, our concept of what is dissonant and what is not has changed. Intervals that were once thought to be quite dissonant now sound consonant to our ears because of repeated usage. In the seventeenth century, however, there were strict and unbending ideas about which intervals were dissonant, and therefore unusable, and those that were consonant and usable. These were as follows:

Consonant intervals:
octave
perfect fifth
major and minor sixths
major and minor thirds

Until the end of the sixteenth century, the octave and fifth were considered "perfect" concords and the others were considered "imperfect" concords. Later, some musicians felt that the major sixth was, in fact, the most consonant of all intervals. Again, it's a matter of taste and judgement.

Dissonant intervals:
major and minor sevenths
major and minor seconds
perfect fourth
all augmented and diminished intervals

▼ What is a triad?

A triad is a combination of three notes sounded at the same time to create a chord. Most chords are based on the foundation of a triad starting with the root, or first note of the chord, the third, and the fifth. A C-major chord is made up of the root, C, the third, E, and the fifth, G. An A-minor chord is also based on the same pattern: the root, A, the third, C, and the fifth, E.

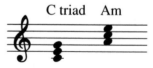

▼ What is a chord?

A chord is a group of three notes *or more* that are sounded at the same time. Almost every chord is created on top of the foundation of a triad. A C-major chord is the same as a C-major triad as both are composed of the same three notes: C-E-G. Many chords are made up of more than three notes, beginning with a major or minor triad and adding notes to it. A C-major triad with a sixth added would be called a C6; A C-major triad with a seventh would be a C7, etc. So while every triad can be considered a chord, not every chord is a triad.

▼ What's the difference between a major chord and a minor chord?

The difference is that a major chord is based on a triad that contains a major third and a minor chord is based on a triad that contains a minor third.

A C-major chord is C-E-G while a *C-minor* chord is C-E flat-G. Both are still triads containing the root, the third, and the fifth. The only difference is that the minor chord has a minor third in it and the major chord has a major third.

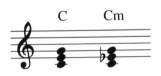

▼ What do you get if you leave out the third altogether and use only the root and the fifth?

You get an interval of a perfect fifth. For example, if you play a C-major chord without the third, you play the notes C and G. This is not really a chord: it's an interval without a third and so is neither major nor minor.

▼ What is a seventh chord?

It is a chord that adds the seventh note of the scale above the triad. There are different kinds of seventh chords, though, depending on if the seventh note is a major seventh or a minor seventh.

For example, the seventh note in the C-major scale is a B natural, which is the major seventh. (The minor seventh is one half step below that: B flat.)

If you play a C-major triad with this B natural above it, you now have a major seventh chord, which we call C major seventh, or simply C maj7. On the piano, play:

C E G B

The sound of a major seventh chord is distinctive, punctuated by the dissonance created by sounding the B natural, which is a half step below the tonic. And even if that upper tonic is not played, it is implied by its octave in the root. This creates the feeling of a minor second—that dissonant rubbing of the C against the B, which is only a half step away.

As you can tell on the piano, the minor second—a B and a C played at the same time—is the most dissonant interval there is. The ear has a hard time distinguishing between two notes that are so close together. However, when you play the same notes but with space between them—a C with a B played in the octave above—you get the sound of the major seventh, which is dissonant, yes, but also quite pleasing to the ear; the space between the notes allows us to hear both of them and the way that they interact.

Perhaps the best example of the use of major seventh chords is Erik Satie's composition *Trois Gymnopedies*. It's a piece you may be familiar with because the rock band Blood, Sweat and Tears did their own version of it. It's a piece based on the interaction of two chords—a I major seventh and a IV major seventh.

Like the key change, though, the major seventh chord is something that can sound quite cliché and corny if overused. But if used with some degree of subtlety, it can add a beauty and a richness to a melody.

One way to do this is by not using the major seventh chord at the beginning of a phrase, but as a passing chord, moving between two chords. We saw earlier how Charlie Chaplin used an F major 7 chord in the second phrase of "Smile." Another good example is the Beatles' song "Something," written by George Harrison. The C major 7 chord is used in the first phrase, after a C-major chord. The first line of the song in "Something in the way she moves . . ." The C-major chord is played until the word "moves," at which time the C major *seventh* chord is played; this is the same point where the melody shifts from a C natural to a B natural, matching the chords. That B natural sung on the word "moves" is the essence of the major seventh effect, clashing peacefully with the sound of the C in the bass.

The next chord in the song is also based on the C-major triad but instead of a major seventh, it has a *flatted* or minor seventh. Instead of a B natural, there is a B flat. The chord is:

C E G B flat

This kind of a chord is called a *dominant seventh* and instead of a major seventh it contains a minor seventh, creating a wholly different sound. To write it, however, we simply leave out the word "major" and write C7. By this we know it is a dominant seventh chord, with a minor and not a major seventh.

In our example song, "Something," it is the third chord in the song, preceding the word "attracts":

C   **Cmaj7**

Something in the way she moves

C7   **F**

Attracts me like no other lover. . . .

The dominant seventh chord has a harsher, less pretty sound than the major seventh chord. It is the chord at the heart of most blues and rock music, adding a bluesy, rough edge to a major triad.

To see what I mean, play, on piano or guitar, the following chord progression:

C /F /C /F /C /G /C

Now try the same kind of progression but make each chord a dominant seventh chord:

C7 /F7 /C7 /F7 /C7 /G7 /C7

The entire sound becomes more jazzy and jaunty, an effect that you can use to your advantage. Again, it's more effective when used sparingly, just as the major seventh chord. Rather than using it in every measure, as in our previous example, you

can slip them in and out of a song and combine them with other chords, as George Harrison did in our example from "Something."

▼ ***Why isn't a dominant seventh called a "minor seventh chord" (it does have a minor seventh in it)?***

The reason we call a dominant seventh chord a C7 instead of a C minor seventh is because it contains a *major* third. The "minor" in a minor seventh chord refers to the minor third, not the minor seventh. A chord symbol that says C minor seventh (or Cm7) means that it is a C-*minor* triad with a minor seventh attached to it:

C E flat G B flat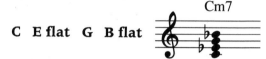

(a C7 chord, remember, is: C E G B flat)
An Am7 chord is an A minor chord with the minor seventh added:

A C E G

And a Dm7 chord is a D minor chord plus the minor seventh:

D F A C

▼ ***What is a "suspended fourth" chord?***

It's a chord that is based on a triad that has a fourth instead of a third. If you were to place an E natural between a C and a G, you would get a C-major chord. An E flat placed there will give you a C-minor chord. And if you put an F natural between a C and a G (the F being an interval of a fourth from the C) you get what is called a "suspended fourth" chord.

A "suspended fourth" is a chord based on the root (C), fourth (F), and the fifth (G). In D, the chord would be spelled D-G-A. It's a suspended chord because it creates tension: the fourth working against the root and the fifth pulling the chord, usually in the direction of resolving to the third. Play the C suspended fourth (C sus 4) and listen to it. See how it is pulling you to resolve it back to a C-major chord? The F, or fourth, leads back to the E, or major third.

Why does it do this? The interval of a fourth (from the C to the F) is not a dissonant interval like a minor second is. However, in a suspended fourth chord like this, the fourth works against the fifth: in this C sus 4 chord you have C-F-G, and the interval between the F and the G (the fourth and the fifth) is a minor second, which creates tension and the need to resolve.

▼ What is a diminished chord?

A diminished chord is a chord that contains a diminished fifth rather than a perfect fifth. The interval from C to G is a perfect fifth; if you diminish it by a half step, from C to G *flat*, you have a diminished fifth.

A diminished chord is based on a triad that has this interval of the diminished fifth—from C to G flat—and in between the fifth a minor third. A C-diminished chord, therefore, is:

C E flat G flat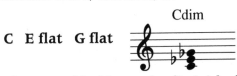

Another way of looking at the diminished chord is that it consists of two minor thirds, from C to E flat and from E flat to G flat: C, E flat, G flat. A diminished chord creates tension and must resolve. Because of its structure, it can resolve in more than one direction. Try experimenting to see where diminished chords lead you. A C-diminished chord, for example, leads to C major, but also to C minor and to B major. For this reason, they are wonderful tools for connecting chords and are often used in key changes.

▼ What is an augmented chord?

An augmented chord is a chord based on a fifth that is enlarged, or augmented, by a half step. Instead of having a minor third in its center (as does

the diminished chord) it has a major third. A C-augmented chord is:

C E G#

It is a chord based on two *major* thirds, as opposed to the diminished chord based on two *minor* chords. Like the diminished chord, the augmented chord is dissonant and creates tension that must resolve. And it can also resolve in different directions. A C-augmented chord (C-E-G#) pulls us towards an F-major chord but can also move to an A minor quite nicely, Experiment with augmented chords to see where they lead you.

▼ Sometimes it seems so predictable to resolve a phrase in a normal way. Are there ways to resolve chords that aren't as obvious?

One technique is to use the deceptive cadence. This is a phrase that ends in a way that the listener would not expect but that works in the key and is not jarring. As an example, play this simple progression in C major, with each chord receiving one measure of time or four beats:

C . . . **/F** . . . **/G** . . . **/C** . . .

This can also be written as:

I . . . **/IV** . . . **/V** . . . **/I** . . .

The V chord, or dominant (G in our example), creates tension and pulls us toward the tonic. In our example, that resolution comes as expected in the fourth measure. That's a normal, nondeceptive cadence. Let's substitute a VI chord, or A minor in this key, instead of the tonic in the fourth measure:

C . . . **/F** . . . **/G** . . . **/A minor**

I . . . **/IV** . . . **/V** . . . **VIm** . . .

This is a deceptive cadence, because the ear expects a return to the tonic and we go instead to the relative minor chord, the A minor. Not only do we hear a different chord than we expected, but because it is a minor chord it jolts the ear in a pleasing way. So anytime that you go to the minor six chord in a cadence instead of tonic, you are utilizing a deceptive cadence.

▼ Can you also do a deceptive cadence while you are in a minor key?

Yes. If you are in a minor key and go to the VI chord, or the relative *major* chord of the key, you also have a deceptive cadence. For example, a I, IV, V, I progression in the key of A minor is as follows:

Am . . . /Dm . . . /E . . . /Am

In the key of A minor, the VI chord is F major, which is the relative major chord of the key. So the progression would go:

Am . . . /Dm . . . /E . . . /F . . .

Try this out and you will see that it's a pretty sound, a nice variation on the old return to the tonic.

Trick chords

Another technique is the use of what composer David Foster has called the "trick chord." This is a chord that is not a deceptive cadence but serves a similar purpose. When the ear expects the progression to return to tonic or a similarly predictable chord, suddenly you go to a new place. (But not the relative major or minor.) To find the trick chord, play your progression and sing the melody you have with it. For example, this progression in C major, again:

C . . . /Am . . . /F . . . /G . . .

And the melody that goes with this progression is extremely simple, a C note held for three measures moving up one tone to a D on the fourth measure, corresponding to the G chord.

To find the trick chord, instead of using the G chord on the fourth measure, move to any other chord that has that same melody note (D) in it. You can go to a D-minor chord:

C . . . /Am . . . /F . . . /Dm

You can go to a D-major chord, which really changes the feel:

C . . . /Am . . . /F . . . /D . . .

or a B-diminished chord, which has the D in the middle (B, D, F):

C . . . /Am . . . /F . . . /B dim . . .

or an E7 chord, in which the D is the seventh note (E, G#, B, D):

C . . . /Am . . . /F . . . /E7 . . .

Try playing each one of these progressions on a keyboard or guitar, and you will see that each matches the melody but each one has a different nature, and leads in a different way to what would be the next chord and the next turn of the melody. So these trick chords can be used as detours to take you in new directions and down different roads than the ones you've traveled before.

▼ What other techniques are there for making chord progressions and cadences more interesting?

A powerful chord to use in a chord progression is the secondary dominant. It is a dominant chord (a V chord) to any chord in a key other than the tonic. As you already know, a dominant chord is a chord built on the fifth tone of any scale. In the key of C major, the dominant is G. G is the V of C, which is I. In this key, G is the primary dominant. A *secondary* dominant refers to a chord that is the V of a chord that is *not* tonic. For example, in C major, the secondary dominant to the II chord, D minor, is A major. An A-major chord isn't a chord in the key of C major as it is comprised of the notes A, C#, and E. A C sharp obviously is not in the key of C major as C major has no sharps. This is the reason the chord calls attention to itself, as there is an unexpected tone in the progression that creates tension and must resolve, in this case, to D minor.

Here are the secondary dominants for chords in C major.

Chord.	Secondary Dominant.
D minor (IIm)	A major (V of II)
E minor (IIIm)	B major V of III)

F major (IV)   C major (V of IV)

G major (V)   D major (V of V)

A minor (VI)   E major (V of VI)

It's common to use a secondary dominant as an effective means of moving to the relative minor chord, the VI chord, of a key. In C the VI chord is A minor. The secondary dominant to A minor is E major. To understand the feeling created by a secondary dominant, play these two progressions. The first leads from C to A minor without the secondary dominant, and the second does use the chord. Notice the difference:

1. C . . . /C . . . /Am . . . /Am . . .

2. C . . . /C . . . /E . . . /Am . . .

See how the placement of the E-major chord adds a new tone to the progression and pushes you toward the A minor? This is the effect of the secondary dominant.

There are countless examples of the use of this chord in popular songs. In fact, you hear it so often you are not aware of it consciously. One of my favorites is from the standard, "When You Wish upon a Star" from *Pinocchio* (Lyrics by Ned Washington and music by Leigh Harline). It occurs in the very first line of the song, which is in C major and moves from C to D minor via the secondary dominant (the V of VI), which is A major in this instance:

C   A   Dm

When   you   wish   upon   a   star

Try playing this line both with and without the use of the secondary dominant (A major) connecting the C and the D minor, and feel the effect. Another instance of its usage is in a song we've already

looked at, "Smile." It was composed by Charlie Chaplin, something few people realize, for his movie *Modern Times*. In the song, which is in F major, Chaplin utilizes a secondary dominant (D major) for the II chord (G minor in the key of F) but makes it even more effective because instead of using it as a passing chord, as in our last example, it is put in a place of rhythmic emphasis where the melody note is found in the secondary dominant itself. It comes after these lines: "Smile, though your heart is aching, smile, even though it's breaking" (see bottom of this page).

The sound is powerful because of the emphasis the chord gets in the song. The F sharp in the D-major chord (D-F#-A) is used in the melody. Since the song is in F natural, having a melody note rest on an F sharp is unusual. (It's that most dissonant of intervals, the minor second, which we discussed earlier.) Yet it is hauntingly beautiful because it is contained within that secondary dominant chord, creating tension and leading to the resolution of the G-minor chord.

There are numerous other examples of songs using the secondary dominant. Let's look at two more examples.

The first is "Yesterday," written by Paul McCartney and John Lennon. Like "Smile," the song is also in F major (see bottom of this page).

The secondary dominant here is the A-major chord (on the word "troubles") that leads to the VI chord in the key of F, D minor. Play the progression as is and also as it would be without the secondary dominant, with an A minor instead of an A major. See how the A major literally lifts up the entire melody, and propels it onward. It creates a tension and release and also a sense of uplifting.

The next song is the Hoagy Carmichael/Stuart

Gorrell classic, "Georgia on My Mind," which is another song in the key of F major.

The opening is similar to that of "Yesterday," beginning with the tonic and moving to the VI through the use of the secondary dominant of VI (V of VI).

About this particular song, Scott Eyerly, a composer and teacher who writes the "ShopTalk" column for *SongTalk*, wrote this: "So distinctive are these three chords that, mystics believe, you need only roll them to conjure up the presence of Ray Charles. The song may be one of the few as familiar for its chord progression as its tune."

Creating new chords

There are many other chords that can lend a richness to your melodies, as well as suggest new turns you might take in them. You can play with chords, alter them, superimpose other chords on top of them, try them with alternate bass notes, and basically mix up the medicine to see what kind of potion you can make. Ultimately, you have to find chords that are pleasing to your ear, and in this way develop your own distinctive style.

Carole King said in *SongTalk*, "It's been widely quoted to me that a four chord with a five bass [an F with C in the bass in the key of C, for example] has been one of my signatures. Musicians have called it 'the Carole King chord' although I didn't originate it. But I did use it a lot."

The use of one interesting chord can set the entire mood for a song. We looked earlier at Mann/Weil/Spector's "You've Lost That Loving Feelin'," the entire feeling of which is set by the opening chord, a C with B flat in the bass. The tension created by that very first chord is resolved gently at first in the verse and then explosively in the chorus.

Using simple chords

It's important to remember that a complex chord progression does not guarantee a strong melody. Many gorgeously melodic songs have been written using only three chords: I, IV, and V. Listen to "Blowing in the Wind" or "Twist and Shout" to hear what can be done with only three chords.

The VI chord, used sparingly, can serve as icing on a pretty tasty cake. Listen to Jimmy Webb's breathtaking "All I Know" (recorded by Art Gar-

funkel on *Angel Clare*) for a great example. Revolving basically around a I-IV-V pattern, the melody ascends to a passionate crescendo on the title, where Webb introduces the VI chord. He explained to *SongTalk* that he found the root of this passion in the Baptist church: ". . . it definitely is out of the Baptist hymnal. It reminds me of what I think is the most beautiful hymnal tune; we sang it as 'Come Now, Fount of Every Blessing.' It's very Appalachian. It's very simple and haunting. So I definitely borrowed on that and used that energy . . ."

To get to the source of the music that moves him emotionally at his core, Webb went to the music that accompanied his childhood. In the same way, you can move toward the different chord progressions and melodies that move you personally, and in doing so create a musical signature for yourself.

Complex chord progressions

Realizing the harmonic complexities of many of the great Motown songs written by the team of Holland-Dozier-Holland, I asked Lamont Dozier how he arrived at his unique blend of chords. This was his answer: "I started stretching chords from fifties' rock and roll in the songs we wrote for Motown. You can stretch a chord out by using ninths, elevenths, and thirteenths. That's what I was doing, revoicing the chords and making it wider and thicker; bringing out the best a chord could possibly give for each particular song I was working on.

"I started fooling around, coming up with different ways to approach a chord, instead of the old standard rock and roll chords, the 'rah-rah' chords as we used to call them, the same old triads. I tried it out on a song called 'Come and Get These Memories' in which I used elevenths and thirteenths by expanding the voicing of the chords. I put hours and hours in listening to records. I'd listen to different ways people would structure songs and voice chords. My ear became very good. Then all of a sudden I started forming my own opinions about the way a song should be."

Take Dozier as an example of a songwriter who did his homework and it paid off. Not only did he pen countless hits back in the sixties ("Stop in the Name of Love," "Baby Love," "Heat Wave," and "You Can't Hurry Love" to name only four), but he continues to do so; recently he wrote "Two Hearts" with Phil Collins.

In the same way, it's wise to study both the songs of today as well as the Motown songs that Dozier and the Holland Brothers used, and songs from previous generations like "Smile" and "Georgia" that used chords in a rainbow of ways rock and roll doesn't usually approach. Listen to jazz records and study jazz progressions for a great source of inventive chord usages. Listen to classical music as much as you can. Listen to world music, the music of other countries. Then digest it, store it in the back of your head, and start writing. As Charlie Parker once said, "Learn everything you can. Then forget it all and play."

And Peter Gabriel had this to say: "I try to fill my head and my ears with all sorts of stuff and then let it settle and filter through. At a certain point it seems like a fruitless activity because you're taking a lot of time and not seeming to get anything. And then slowly, you realize you've actually digested elements and that your thinking is freed up and the way you build compositions is changed as a result of what you've been listening to."

▼ What is harmony?

Harmony can refer to a few different musical ideas. On one level, harmony refers to the combination of notes that form intervals and chords. On another level, it refers to the whole science of combining intervals to form chords. When we speak about the way a melody is supported by chord changes, for example, we are discussing the harmony.

In songwriting, though, harmony refers both to the chords that are used as well as to an alternate melodic line that is sung with the melody. It is not meant to be heard as prominently as the melody but to support and enhance the melody.

▼ Is a harmony line always sung higher than the melody line?

No. Harmony can be created by singing a musical line in close intervals to the melody that is either above or below the melody. A great example of both kinds of harmony is just about any song by Simon and Garfunkel. Since Paul and Art grew up together in Queens, New York, they began singing harmony at a young age and perfected the process of combining their voices into two-part harmony. And their harmonies used both methods — having the harmony above the melody and having it below. (A lot of their harmonic prowess came from their devotion to the records of the Everly Bothers, another excellent source of great harmonizing.)

An example of a lower harmony part in which the melody is on the top is Simon and Garfunkel's first hit song, "The Sound of Silence." In this song, Garfunkel sings the melody and Simon sings a harmony line that is *lower* than the melody. This song can be found in two forms. The most well-known version of the song is the rock version that is the title song of the *Sounds of Silence* album.

But the original acoustic version of the song can be found on their first album, *Wednesday Morning, 3AM*. In the original version, sung only against a quiet guitar, it is easiest to hear Simon's lower harmony part, which is on the left side of the stereo. If you get this version, listen to it on a stereo and turn your balance all the way to the left. In this way, it will be easy to hear Simon's harmony part, which is based on only a few notes. Heard alone, Simon's part sounds strange and surprising because it is not the melody but a part created to support the melody. Turn the balance on your stereo back to the center so that you hear Garfunkel's part as well and you can hear how perfectly Simon's harmony part works.

To hear an example of a harmony part that is *higher* than the melody, listen to Simon and Garfunkel's song "The Boxer" from the *Bridge Over Troubled Water* album. In this song, Simon sings the melody line and Garfunkel sings a higher harmony part. The song begins only with Simon, singing: "I am just a poor boy though my story's seldom told . . ." Garfunkel comes in with a higher harmony on the line "All lies and jest . . ." Garfunkel's part is based on the interval of a third, one of the most common intervals on which to base a higher harmony.

Of course, harmony for a melody can have both a higher and a lower harmony. A three-part harmony can have the melody in the middle, with harmony both above and below the melody. Listen to Peter, Paul & Mary or Crosby, Stills & Nash for examples of this. And there is no limit to how many harmony parts a piece can have. To hear four-part harmony singing, listen to any barbershop quartet.

▼ What is rhythm?

Rhythm, which comes from the Latin word for "flow" is the pattern of notes in time and is determined by the length of the notes, the tempo, and the specific arrangement of the notes. It combines meter (the time value of the notes), tempo (the rate of speed of a piece), and beat (which notes are accented).

▼ What is meant by "the meter" that a song is in?

The meter of a song refers to its pattern of beats and the way that pattern is split into measures. Almost all of the music we hear, including songs, is split into measures of equal length so that if a piece is said to be in four, that means it is divided into measures that each receive four beats. The meter of a song or composition is indicated by the time signature.

▼ What is a measure in music?

A measure is a group of beats that repeats throughout a composition and that are separated by bar lines. Each group has the same duration of time in a piece. If a piece is in 4/4, for example, each measure lasts for four beats before the next measure of four beats begins. If a piece is in 3/4 time, then each measure lasts for the duration of three beats.

▼ What is a time signature?

A time signature is a symbol made up of two numbers, one above the other, that tells you what meter a song or composition is in.

The time signature can be found at the beginning of a musical transcription of a piece after the key signature, which comes right after the clef sign.

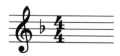

In a time signature, the number on the top refers to how many beats are in each measure. The number on the bottom refers to the time value of the note that gets the beat.

For example, let's look at a common time signature that we call four-four time and is represented by this symbol: 4/4. In 4/4 time, the upper four refers to the number of beats in each measure: four. The lower number refers to the time value that the note gets: here each quarter note (represented by the four) will receive one beat. Therefore, in 4/4 time, there are four quarter notes to each measure.

In 3/4 time, there are *three* quarter notes to each measure. This time is often referred to as "waltz time" as all waltzes are in three.

Most rock songs are written in a meter of either two or four. As Sting commented, most people don't write in three anymore because few people are waltzing these days. As almost all rock songs are in four, even writing a song in 3/4 time or 6/8 time makes for an unusual song these days. Still, Sting's beautiful song "Children's Crusade" is in 3/4 time, and while it might not be ideal for dancing, it has a gorgeous melody with equally stunning lyrics (on his *Dream of the Blue Turtles* album).

In 2/4 time, there are *two* quarter notes to each measure.

In 2/2 time, there are still *two* beats to every measure, but the two on the bottom indicates that the *half note* gets the beat. So in 2/2 time, there are two half notes to every measure.

In 6/8 time, there are *six eighth-notes* to every measure. The sound of 6/8 time, since it is split into six beats (two groups of three), is similar to 3/4 time.

These are the most common time signatures for songs nowadays, but other time signatures that are used are:

3/2, 3/8, 3/16, 4/8, 5/4, 7/8, 9/16, and **12/8.**

Anytime you use a time signature that splits measures into odd-numbered fragments other than three, the sound will be unusual because our ears are accustomed to regular repeating patterns of two or three (even 4/4 is processed in our brains as two groups of two, and similarly, 6/8 is processed as two groups of three). So a song in 5/4, which has five quarter notes to each measure, will sound a little exotic because it is uneven—a group of two and then three (or three then two).

An example of a song in 5/4 time is the theme from "Mission Impossible." To split a measure into five throws us off a little bit. Using odd time signatures like this one is an interesting way to jar yourself into creating something new, something you've never tried before.

An example of a song in 7/4 time, in which there are seven quarter notes to each measure is Peter Gabriel's beautiful "Solsbury Hill" (from his first solo album). This song is a perfect example of a beautiful melody, with astounding lyrics about magic and illusion, written to an unusual time signature. It's so masterfully written that the 7/4 time does not stand out, and you might not even notice it if it weren't pointed out. But the effect is almost hypnotic, rocking back and forth between counts of three and four, underlining the power of the words. Another, and perhaps better known, example of a song in 7/4 time is Pink Floyd's "Money."

A great example of another song in an unusual time signature is "Have a Good Time" by Paul Simon (from *Still Crazy After All These Years*). The song is essentially a blues, revolving around a simple chord progression (a I-IV-I-V progression). What distinguishes it musically, though, is that the verses are in 7/8 time. With each measure split into seven beats, the effect is like hearing a measure of four beats switching off with a measure of three beats, and so on.

▼ Can a song have more than one time signature? Is it possible to start in 4/4, for example, and then switch to 3/4?

Yes. There's no rule that you have to stay in one time signature. Just as you can change keys in midsong (via a mutation or a modulation) you switch from one meter to another by writing in the musical transcription the new time signature at the beginning of the new phrase. In our previous example of Simon's "Have a Good Time," the verse is in 7/8 time. The chorus of the song is in four,

which amplifies that slightly off-center feeling of the verses.

Another example of this is the Beatles' song "We Can Work It Out." (*Yesterday . . . and Today*). The entire song—verses, chorus, and bridge—is in 4/4 except for one section, which comes in the middle of the bridge. The bridge begins with "Life is very short and there's no time/For fussing and fighting my friend . . ." Toward the end of the second and fourth line of the bridge, the meter changes from four to three, first on the words "fighting my friend" and then again on "ask you once again." The time signature at that point is 6/8, which gives the feeling of three instead of four. Listen again to this song to experience the effect.

A good challenge for a beginning songwriter would be to attempt to write a song in which there is a change of meter. But don't do it arbitrarily; work the meter change into a part of the song where it makes sense, such as where the emphasis shifts in the lyrics. Not only is it a challenge to move into the change of meter, but returning to the original meter is another challenge that will force the writer to be inventive so that the return to the original meter sounds natural and unforced.

▼ ————————————————————

"We Can Work It Out" is one of the best examples of Lennon and McCartney's combined genius. Written back in the days when Paul and John would actually write songs together rather than apart, McCartney wrote both the verse and the optimistic chorus of "We can work it out," which essentially states that everything is okay and there's no need to worry. Lennon, who wrote the bridge, brings in a more realistic and less optimistic tone to the song with "Life is very short and there's no time for fussing and fighting . . ." It's a great illustration of how two people's individual outlooks can add up to a complete and integrated song.

———————————————————— ▲

▼ What determines how fast a piece is played? Is 3/4 time, since it has fewer beats to a measure, faster than 4/4 time?

No. The speed at which a song is played has to do with the tempo of the song. The songwriter, or composer, determines the tempo, although a producer might suggest a different tempo, as in, "That's nice, but let's try it just a bit faster."

▼ What is tempo?

Tempo, which comes from the Latin word "tempus" for time, is the rate of speed at which a song, or composition, is played. If it's in 4/4, for example, it can be a slow 4/4, with each measure taking a long time, or a fast 4/4 in which each measure goes by quickly.

▼ How do you indicate the tempo of a song?

You can to it simply by using English words, such as "slow, moderate, fast" at the top of the musical transcription, or you can use the following Italian terms:

Adagio: slow
Allegretto: quick
Andante: moderate
Grave: very slow
Largo: slow
Presto: fast

▼ What is syncopation?

It's the alteration of the normal beat, or accent, of a piece of music. It's experienced as a temporary shift of rhythm that is caused by emphasizing a weak beat.

For example, in most pop or rock songs that are in 4/4 time, the accent is put on the second and fourth beat of each measure, which is the back beat:

1 & 2 & 3 & 4 & / 1 & 2 & 3 & 4 & /

Syncopation would alter that accent so that instead of falling on two and four, it might fall on the eighth note after two and four, as follows:

1 & 2 & 3 & 4 & / 1 & 2 & 3 & 4 &

Or to get even more syncopated, it might fall in the cracks between those notes. Syncopation is a way of working against the rhythm of a piece to add rhythmic variation.

▼ How do you indicate how loud or soft to play a song?

Again, you can use simple English terms such as "loud" and "soft" or you can use the Italian phrases that indicate not only the volume, but with what expression a piece, or song, should be performed (some have abbreviations, such as *p* for piano, as follows):

p — piano: soft
mp — mezzo piano: fairly soft
pp — pianissimo: very soft
f — forte: loud
mf — mezzo forte: fairly loud
ff — fortissimo: very loud

Animato: lively, animated
Con anima; with soul or feeling
Con brio: with spirit
Cantabile: singingly
Cantando: singingly
Expressivo: expressive
Giusto: exact or strict time
Grazioso: graceful
Legato: smoothly
Marcato: accented
Sostenuto: sustained
Staccato: detached
Vivace: vivacious

▼ Why would the word "piano" mean soft? My piano gets pretty loud at times.

The word "piano" does mean soft. The name for the instrument that you are referring to originally was "piano-forte" which literally means soft-loud. It was called this because of its ability to play both loud and soft depending on how it was played (it's touch sensitive, as we would say nowadays), a quality which previous keyboard instruments, such as the harpsichord and the clavichord, did not possess.

▼ *What is improvisation in music?*

Improvisation comes from the Latin word "improvisus" that means "unforeseen." Improvisation in music is the act of spontaneous creation, either in performance, by yourself, or with other musicians. The root of the word—unforeseen—is apt, as you are dealing with the unforeseen, you are playing music that doesn't exist until you play it.

Improvisation can be used while writing and while performing. When writing—especially if you write with other musicians—you can freely improvise (or "jam," a term more frequently used) simply to see what comes out of it, to generate ideas but to do so in the spirit of play, enjoying the music rather than attempting to control it. Phil Collins, who writes most of the songs for his band Genesis with the other members of the band, uses this method, as he told *SongTalk*: "It all stems from im-provisation. When you're improvising, you don't even know if you're going to get something unless you take chances, and that means obviously play-ing bum notes and singing out of tune because you're trying to do something you haven't done before, and that's a chemistry you need to find; that happy blend of people you don't mind being a twit in front of."

Improvisation is the essence of jazz: taking a written melody and experimenting with the varia-tions.

In performance, and while recording, improvi-sation in the midst of a written and arranged song can add a lot of zest and fire. It's easy to get too wrapped up in having firm control of every facet of your production. And this concentration will pro-duce a clean and tight presentation. However, add a sax solo or a guitar solo in the midst of this ar-rangement and suddenly you have brought the en-tire production to a new level.

Song Structure

4

▼ **What is meant by song structure? Can't I structure a song any way that I choose?**

Sure you can. That doesn't mean that there aren't basic song structures, or song forms, you can learn that will help you in your writing. Although there are no rules to songwriting and no required structures, learning the most common structures can be beneficial. It's tantamount to an architect learning the basics of building constructions: one must know what is common and normally done before getting adventurous and stretching the boundaries.

A song structure refers to the arrangement of the component sections of a song. There are three basic sections: the verse, the chorus, and the bridge. A song structure is that combination of these sections that you use to create your song.

▼ **What are the most common song structures?**

The two most common song structures—those you will hear in most songs that are on the radio or on records today—are the verse/chorus structure and the verse/bridge structure.

▼ **What is a verse?**

Verse, which comes from the Latin word for "turning," is a word used in poetry, referring to a metrical line of language, or a stanza. In songs, the verse usually opens the song and has a metrical pattern that is repeated throughout a song with different words each time. So while the metrical pattern and the melody of a verse repeat, the words of a verse change each time.

A good example is Carole King's beautiful song "You've Got a Friend." The song begins:

When you're down and troubled and you need some love and care
And nothing, nothing is going right . . .

That is the first verse of the song.

A main function of the verse is to set the scene of the song. It gives the basic information contained within—a main character, a situation, a tone. It sets the stage, adding more information each time it occurs. The first verse of "You've Got a Friend" establishes the voice: it's written to comfort a friend in need. It begins with direct advice to this person: When you're down, think of me, and I will comfort you. The chorus then extends and encapsulates that same idea.

▼ **What is a chorus?**

The chorus is the section of the song that repeats both musically and lyrically. It is the section that almost always contains the title of the song, often at the beginning of the chorus and sometimes at the end of the chorus. In "You've Got a Friend" the chorus extends the verse as the singer promises no matter when she is needed she will be there, and it leads to the title and main idea of the song: "You just call out my name and you know wherever I am, I'll come running to see you again/ Winter, spring, summer or fall, all you've got to do is call and I'll be there/You've got a friend."

In many songs, the verse melody builds up to the chorus, creating a certain tension that is relieved by the "release" of the chorus. We examined this tension/release process at the heart of "You've Lost That Lovin' Feelin' " in which the verses build up to the release of the chorus lyrically, melodically, and harmonically.

▼ What is a verse/chorus structure?

That is a song structure consisting of verses and choruses. Usually the song begins with at least one verse, often two, and is followed by the chorus. Then the structure repeats itself with one or more verses and another chorus. There is no limit to this: some folk songs go on to include twenty verses, always repeating the same chorus each time.

"You've Got a Friend" is written in the verse/ chorus structure. The verses employ the same melody and metric structure each time but with different lyrics; the chorus remains the same each time and is repeated after the verses.

▼ What is meant by an AABA structure or an ABABCB structure?

When you see letters like that they are defining what kind of structure the song has. A verse/bridge structure is labeled AABA with the letter A referring to the verse and B standing for the bridge. Therefore, AABA means that the song has one verse, then another verse, a bridge, and another verse.

ABABCB refers to a verse/chorus structure. Here the A stands for the verse, the B stands for the chorus, and the C stands for the bridge. Hence, ABABCB means verse, chorus, verse, chorus, bridge, chorus.

Any song structure can be detailed in this way. For example, a structure that is AABAABCB means verse, verse, chorus, verse, verse, chorus, bridge, chorus. As an exercise, try to apply identifying letters to one of your own songs or a song that you enjoy.

When someone refers to the "A section" or the "B section" of a song, they are using this method of assigning a letter to each section of a song.

▼ In a song structure, what is a bridge?

A bridge, in a song, is similar to the kind of bridge that connects two areas of land. In a song, the bridge is a section that is neither a verse nor a chorus but is used to connect verses with verses, verses with choruses, or choruses with choruses. A bridge usually does not contain the title of a song, though it can. Its main function is to step away from the structure for a moment, and to offer another angle on the song both musically and lyrically.

A bridge can be used in a verse/chorus structure, where it often is placed between the last two repeats of the chorus to break up the pattern and to make each chorus sound more exciting. It's a deviation from the repetitive verse/chorus structure, and can add a different perspective to the song.

"You've Lost That Lovin' Feelin' " also serves as a good example of a bridge. It's the section starting with "Baby, baby, I get down on my knees for you . . . " It provides a detour in which the beat shifts slightly and new material, both musical and lyrical, is added. This bridge, however, does differ from many bridges in that it's rather long (twenty-six measures). Often bridges are no longer than eight measures, the reason that they are also referred to sometimes as "the middle eight."

A bridge is also necessary in the verse/bridge structure.

▼ What is the verse/bridge structure?

This is the song structure that has no chorus and revolves around the uses of verses that have the title contained within them, and a bridge. It's also referred to as the AABA structure, in which the A sections, or verses, are alike while the B section, or bridge, is different. In this structure, the title often comes at the end of the verse and the entire verse leads up to it both musically and lyrically. The bridge then serves as a release from that pattern.

For example, let's look at the song "Still Crazy

After All These Years" by Paul Simon, from the album of the same name. This is a song in a verse/bridge structure. It has three verses, all ending with the title. The first verse begins with, "I met my old lover on the street last night . . ." and ends with, "still crazy after all these years . . ." Even though the song has no chorus it does have what can be considered a hook, and that is the use of the title at the end of each verse repeated twice. Simon sets up the title by providing a rhyme for "years" with the word "beers." When working in this structure, you often have to set up the title with a different rhyme each time. In the next verse of the song he sets up the title with "Whisper in my ears."

In between the second and the third verse comes another section, one that is neither a verse nor a chorus. What is it? Why, the bridge, of course! It is a section that occurs only once in the song and that has its own metric pattern and its own melody. It is the section that begins with, "Four in the morning/Crapped out, yawning/Longing my life away . . ." This section provides a relief from the repetition of the verses and the verse pattern. It provides a new lyrical direction. And musically it is entirely fresh, offering a strong contrast to the verse melody that strengthens the sound of the verse when we return to it.

Paul Simon, being one of the true masters of the American song, invested even more of a contrast in the bridge by only using notes in the bridge that hadn't been used elsewhere in the song. While you don't have to go to that length to ensure that the bridge will be refreshing (and I know not another example of any songwriter using that method), you can use your bridge as a strong contrast to the other sections of your song, both musically and lyrically.

▼ Is the chorus the same as the hook?

"Hook" is a somewhat unfortunate term often used by music publishers and others who market music. It refers to the part of the song that "hooks" the listener, which is usually the chorus or title section of the song. In "Let It Be," the hook refers to almost the entire chorus. In other songs, the hook might be part of a chorus, the part containing the title and the most climactic musical treatment. Other times the hook can actually be a repeating instrumental riff, such as in the song "Baker Street" by Gerry Rafferty, in which the hook is a melody played on the saxophone. Whatever comprises the hook, it is always the most catchy, memorable musical section of a song, the part that you would later find yourself humming.

A publisher might listen to a song of yours that has a clear chorus and say, "This song has no hook." By that, he doesn't mean the song has no chorus, but that it hasn't got a chorus that was strong enough to hook him in. So when a publisher uses the phrase "hook" he is referring not only to the chorus, but to how catchy and memorable it is.

Most publishers listen to a song only once; often they don't even listen to the whole song. Therefore, if the chorus isn't strong enough on only one listening, they'll say it has no hook or that the hook is weak. If you are writing songs for other artists and pitching them to publishers (as opposed to writing songs for yourself as an artist), it's advisable to be familiar with what a hook is and how to write one.

▼ What's an example of a strong hook?

A good example is contained in the song that made Madonna famous, "Like a Virgin." Written by the team of Billy Steinberg and Tom Kelly, the chorus of the song is: "Like a virgin/touched for the very first time. . . ." It's a strong hook because it's extremely memorable both lyrically and musically: you hear it once and it gets in your head. Just the use of the word "virgin" is enough to make the lyric stand out, and that coupled with a simple but catchy melody adds up to a strong hook.

What actually defines a strong hook is taste. What do you like about your favorite songs? Do they have a repeating section that hooks you in? Listen to five of your favorites and try to analyze what it was that first attracted you to them. Was it a lyric, a melody, or some combination of both? When you have done that, try to write a song that matches that same quality, a song that can accomplish emotionally what your favorite songs accomplish.

5

Collaboration

▼ *I don't write music but I write song lyrics. Should I consider myself a songwriter?*

Yes, but a songwriter in need of a collaborator. A song is a combination of words and music; words without music are lyrics. So while you can consider yourself a songwriter, essentially you are a *lyricist*.

This is not to imply that you can't have great success as a lyricist. Many of those who have made the greatest contributions to the art of songwriting have been lyricists who wrote no music: Ira Gershwin, E. Y. "Yip" Harburg, Alan Jay Lerner, Johnny Mercer, Lorenz Hart, and Bernie Taupin, to name only a few. As a lyricist you can have a long, fruitful career. But it does certainly depend on finding the right person or people with whom to collaborate.

If you are a composer who writes no words, you are also in need of a collaborator if you want a career in songwriting. You can write instrumentals, of course, and you can also move into other fields of instrumental writing, such as scoring for films and TV and writing for orchestras and other ensembles. But to write more mainstream, commercial songs, you'll want to collaborate with a lyricist.

Working with a collaborator is also beneficial for people who write both words and music. Often a collaborator can add a new angle or perspective to a song, moving into areas you might never have considered, both lyrically and musically. If you are an expert with soft ballads, for example, working with someone who writes killer R&B songs can challenge you and help you expand your artistic sense.

If you are someone accustomed to writing both the words and music by yourself, working with a collaborator might require some adjustment on your part. You will no longer be the only one in charge of the song; your collaborator might have different ideas about it than you do. You will have to learn to bend artistically sometimes, and come to certain compromises.

▼ *How do I find a collaborator?*

There are a variety of ways. The best way is to see if there are any songwriter associations in your city or nearby, and if they offer song workshops. If so, these are ideal places for meeting other people in your position, either composers in need of lyricists or vice versa. In a workshop you have the opportunity to let the group hear your work and the chance to hear their work. In this way you can find a collaborator who is a kindred soul artistically.

Many songwriter groups offer some kind of collaborator network as well. The National Academy of Songwriters (NAS) has what it calls the "Songwriter's Network." This is published in each issue of *SongTalk* newspaper, and it is a listing of people around the country looking for collaborators. Any member of NAS can use this service, no matter where you live.

For more information on all aspects of collaboration, I suggest that you pick up a copy of Walter

Carter's excellent book, *The Songwriter's Guide to Collaboration*, published by Writer's Digest Books as part of their Songwriter's Market Business Series.

▼ Does my collaborator have to live in the same city as I do?

No. Collaboration by mail is not only possible, it is common. Nowadays people are quickening the process by using fax machines to send songs back and forth. And with the advent of the computer age, collaborating on computers—sending lyrics and music to a collaborator by the use of a modem—will soon be commonplace.

But how effective can this collaboration be if the two writers never meet face-to-face to work? That depends on the two individuals. Some people prefer a collaboration in which the two writers work simultaneously, inspiring each other to spontaneously create and to build a momentum by that teaming of energies. And many great songs have been written this way: Goffin and King often wrote songs together at the same time; and Lennon and McCartney, in the earliest days of their collaboration, were known to sit face to face while putting songs together.

Other writers, though, need time alone to generate creativity. And this means taking a lyrical idea, or a melodic one, and working on it in solitude, emerging only when a piece is complete. If you are this type of writer who can work alone better than in the presence of another person, then collaboration by mail or other means could be ideal for you.

▼ What should I look for in a collaborator?

Most importantly you want to find someone who has similar tastes in music, and similar goals and motivations for writing songs.

The reason is that for a songwriting collaboration to work well, two people must write like one person. You are, after all, trying to create a work that can and often is created by a single person. There must be a "marriage" between the words and the music, and for two people to pull that off, their chemistry has to be very compatible. Some of the greatest songwriting teams of all times have been married couples: Goffin & King, Mann &

Weil, Ashford & Simpson are only three. Others have been brothers, like the Gershwins, while others, like Lennon and McCartney, spent so much time together from an early age that they were almost like brothers. When there is dissension among collaborators, that is usually when the strong songs cease to be written and when the team breaks up.

While the musical tastes of collaborators needn't be identical, they should at least be complementary. A folk writer, for example, might work quite nicely with a country writer or even a rock writer. But if one writer likes heavy metal primarily and the other is a Neil Sedaka fan, chances are that their collaboration will not be a mutually satisfactory one.

Songwriters are usually quite willing to declare which writers they appreciate and which they feel are overrated. This is a quick and easy method for determining the tastes of a potential collaborator. If they begin praising a writer you deplore, or cutting down one of your favorites, there's no need to begin a collaboration that might be fruitless.

And regardless of the musical tastes of collaborators, sometimes simply the personal chemistry between two people will determine if a collaboration might work. Is this somebody you can talk to easily? Does the person understand you? Do you understand him or her? Do you want to spend much time with this person? Any time? Would you be able to stand your ground with this person over disagreements? Is she or he funny, boring, colorful, vague?

And what are your potential collaborator's motivations in writing songs? This is also easily determined when talking music. If he praises songs on the basis of chart position or sales as opposed to their artistic merit, that is a good tip-off that he is more concerned with writing a hit than writing a song. Does she like any songwriters not in the Top 40? Is she trying to imitate trends or attempting to do something individual? Collaborations will be more successful when both writers have the same goal in mind for their songs.

▼ Should collaborators bother to sign a contract with each other?

Yes. It is wise to have some kind of agreement with your collaborator before you begin to collaborate seriously, so that both parties are adequately protected. Sometimes artistic differences can become so great that it separates writing partners, and questions of authorship arise. How does one party prove that he contributed to a song? After a song is complete how does anyone really know who wrote what? To ensure that you receive the credit for all work that you complete, make sure you have a clear agreement with your collaborator at the start simply to protect both of you.

As Elvis Costello said about his collaboration with Paul McCartney when asked how much input each writer had, "It's not like there's a secretary sitting there with a notepad writing down, 'Then Mr. McCartney suggested the use of a B-flat minor.'" For that reason, McCartney and his former collaborator, John Lennon, made an agreement when they were young that all songs written by them, together or separately, would list "Lennon & McCartney" as writers. At the time, John and Paul were following in the tradition of great songwriting teams that came before them, and specifically their idols, Goffin and King.

▼ ————————————————

The National Academy of Songwriters has prepared a Collaborator's Agreement Contract. Here are the guidelines for that contract:

Checkpoints for the Contents of Collaborator's Agreements

"A handshake isn't good enough, even among the best of friends. Things can change among friends and relatives. Songs are tangible property that can be willed, sold, or assigned. If a writer dies, heirs assume ownership of a copyright and may have different feelings about things than the original owner. Copyrights are often the subject of contract lawsuits and probates. The list below is designed to give you the guidelines for important points:

1. Label the agreement: 'Collaborator's Songwriter Agreement.'
2. Identify all parties: name, address, and Social Security number.
3. Identify the composition(s).
4. Identify who writes the lyrics and who writes the music. (If both write both, or some combination thereof, clearly designate.)
5. Designate exact percentages to each writer for royalties collected and for expenses incurred (usually the same proportion).
6. Provide for the possibility of another cowriter being brought in later, such as for a foreign language lyric or new musical arrangement, and how the percentage of royalties will be changed.
7. Provide the power of attorney to both parties so that if one writer is out of town for an extended period or is impossible to locate, the other(s) can convey the copyright. This necessitates notarizing the agreement.
8. Provide that if a collaborator is dissatisfied at any point up to the signing of the song to a third party, the collaborator may withdraw his or her contribution to the work, provided no claim is made to the remaining song (this isn't always possible).
9. State whether each, both, or neither writer may make future changes, or whether changes need to be mutually agreed upon.
10. Provide for the arbitration of disputes, either through NAS or another group or individual, and make the decision of that party binding on all collaborators.
11. Date and sign the agreement: if power of attorney is given, have the agreement notarized.

This checklist is merely a guideline in preparing simple agreements with cowriters. It is not intended as legal advice or as a substitute for having a competent attorney draft an agreement. For agreements which establish exclusive writing relationships, consult a member of the NAS legal panel."

———————————————— ▲

Another matter to consider when making a collaborator's agreement is the use of songs in contests. Lately there are so many song contests that some songwriters have entered songs without the consent of cowriters. In one instance a song was entered by a cowriter whose contribution to the song was minimal, at best, and who never alerted his collaborator when that song won first prize.

Make sure that in your agreement there is a clause designating that all cowriters agree before a song is entered in any contest, and that all writers will split potential prize money into the same percentages that royalties are split into. If your contribution to a song was small and you receive an agreed-upon 10 percent of the royalties, that is the same percentage you would receive of any prize money.

▼ What is meant by a marriage between words and music?

When songwriters talk about a marriage between the words and music of a song, they are talking about a *good* marriage, a marriage in which both parts are equal, in which neither overshadows the other.

A good marriage between the words and the music of a song is what makes a song succeed. If the words are brilliant and the music is pedestrian, the song will not be effective. Rather than the good words making the music sound better, the music will make the words seem worse. Similarly, a good melody—even a great one—with okay words will only be an okay song and not a great one. A songwriter, whether working alone or with a collaborator, must strive to see that neither the words nor the music of the song show any shortcomings.

Words that sing well

But what is meant by a "good melody" or "brilliant words"? Lyrics that seem brilliant on their own can be totally wrong for a certain melody if they draw too much attention to themselves. A wonderful poem, for example, does not make a good song lyric. A lyric has to have many things: meaning, brevity, a rhyme scheme, a good use of sound, etc. Whereas a Dylan Thomas poem might be exquisitely beautiful to read, or to hear spoken, try singing one. It won't be easy, and the reason is that some words simply do not sing well; they do not work easily when set to music. Therefore, when writing words to a melody or words that will be set to music, you must be conscious of choosing words that sing well, that flow in terms of melody, and that do not sound awkward or clunky when matched to a melody. And as time goes on and you write many songs, you will become familiar with

those words that are pleasing to the ear and that can be sung well, and those that do not work well in a song.

Certain vowel sounds are pleasing to hear, depending on the voice. The sound of a long "I" can be quite pleasing when sustained in the voice, as in "Smile" and other songs.

Paul Simon has admitted a special preference for certain vowel sounds as well as some consonants. He said that he likes *G*s and *L*s as well as the percussive nature of hard consonants like *K*s and *T*s. If you listen to any of his recordings, you can hear in his enunciation a concentration on these sounds. An example of this is from the last verse of his song "The Boxer" (from *Bridge Over Troubled Water*): ". . . and he carries the reminders of every glove that laid him down/Or cut him till he cried out . . ." The highlighting of the hard *C*s on "cut him" and "cried out" is carried in the voice and amplified in the percussion, emphasizing the anger and hurt contained in the lyric.

Good prosody

Another consideration is how words are naturally accented in speech. And few things sound worse than when a word is accented incorrectly in a song. Say you are using the word "eventually" in a song. The accent in that word falls on the second syllable, the "vent." If your melody accents the word in any other place, such as on the third syllable of the word ("tu"), it will sound entirely wrong and forced to the ear. You have to be conscious to set the words in a way that they sound conversational, unforced, and natural.

For there to be a good marriage between the words and the music, the words should complement and not oppose the music (and vice versa). The words must fit in with the rhythm of the music, and the places where the tune rises and falls; when the music moves toward a climax, the words, too, should explode.

As an example, let's look again at Carole King's "You've Got a Friend." The rhythm of the song is moderate and soothing, matching a message of devoted friendship. The chorus builds and rises to its most climactic point on the lines: "You know wherever I am, I'll come running . . ." and then descends slightly to the title line, "You've got a friend." In this way the title is almost an afterthought, serving as the emotional base of the entire song; the underpinning holding up the message of the lyric.

Carol Bayer Bacharach, who is now both the wife and main collaborator of Burt Bacharach, spoke at a *SongTalk* seminar about the genius of Hal David, Bacharach's previous lyricist. She said that David was even more brilliant than people realize because he made Bacharach's melodies seem easy and simple when in fact they are quite complex. David's lyrics matched the music so perfectly that one does not notice how unusual and sophisticated Bacharach's melodies actually are. Listen to one of his songs like "Alfie," for example, and you will hear a melody that is anything but simple. Many of the phrases end with a diminished chord where the ear expects the finality of a major chord. The first phrase begins with the tonic, C, and moves to the II chord, a Dm7, which is used frequently to move to the V chord and then back to tonic. Instead of doing this and going where the ear expects to go, Bacharach travels to an F# diminished chord that pulls the carpet out from under us before returning to the Dm7. The cadence ends on an ambiguous note, an A, which is the sixth in the key of C, and leaves us hanging before beginning the next phrase and extending the melody in a wistful way. David matched the sentiment contained in this progression perfectly by shaping the phrase into a question, so that the nonresolution of the cadence supports the unresolved and searching nature of the words:

no longer seems complex, it simply seems *right*.

As in a marriage between people, an ideal marriage between words and music is one in which both parties bring out the best in each other. Where a melody seems awkward, the lyrics should be smooth. Where lyrics need strength, the music should be strong.

Writing words to music

When writing words to a melody, it's important to write words that fit that specific melody, not simply words that are brilliant on their own. There should never be a sense that words are imposed on a melody, and that the two don't naturally go together. You are attempting to put together two disparate forces in the hope of uniting them into one entity. If one of those forces is too strong, it will overwhelm the other. How many beautiful melodies have become quickly forgettable due to a prosaic lyric?

Of course, writing suitable words to a beautiful melody is no easy feat. It's easy to come up with words that aspire toward beauty and arrive instead at triteness. And at the same time, it's easy to go in the other direction and write words that are too original or clever or unusual for a melody, and in doing so, distract from the power of the song.

There are many different ways of approaching writing words to a melody. One way is to listen to the melody many times with no intention of thinking up words that will fit it. Instead, simply listen to what the melody says to you. What is it about? What feelings does it create in you? What

With a masterfully written lyric, a lyric that matches the ebbs and flows of the tune, the song takes on an organic quality in which the melody

pictures does it paint? Is it a love song? Is there a time, a place, a person? After doing this, jot down these ideas and see if you can form any kind of structure for the content of the song. Then follow this up by creating a story containing the specifics you have discovered, being as specific as possible. Establish a strict sense of time, place, and character.

Then forget all about your intended meaning. In the words of David Byrne, "stop making sense." Instead, listen to the melody and try to imagine what sounds work well with the movement of the tune. See if those sounds suggest any words or phrases. If so, write them down with no attention given to what they mean or if they fit into your context. Let the music write the song for you; let it show you where certain sounds are needed.

When Paul Simon put English lyrics to the African music that eventually became the songs on his *Graceland* album, he paid great attention to the sounds of the original African lyrics, and his lyrics were based on those sounds. He then fashioned the meaning of the songs around those beginning sound placements. In the same way, listen to what sounds your melody requires, and base your lyrics on those qualities.

After that process is complete, look at the lines in front of you. See if they connect in any way themselves, if there is any inner logic that links them. Then see if they connect in any way with the intended meaning of the song, the details you jotted down earlier. To do this well you have to keep your mind open and look for new connections between things you may have never thought of before. The rest is like putting together a puzzle, connecting the different parts until they all fit into one organic whole. Dig deep into your imagination, and you can come up with some brilliant solutions.

It's true that to write a cohesive, understandable song a writer should concentrate on a main idea, a single concept if you will. But to expand on the idea metaphorically and to discover inventive linguistic ways of expressing that concept, your mind will often provide you with images or ideas that at first seem unrelated to the subject at hand. It's similar to a dream in which people and places and things get all mixed up that don't seem to belong together. Yet the mind provides these mixed images and ideas precisely because there is a connection.

A technique used in poetry seminars to help writers find these connections is one that's also useful when beginning a lyric. Write down four verbs, four nouns, and four adjectives. Then write a few verses about a single subject—winter, for example—in which you try to use all of these words. Use other words as well, but see in which direction your list of twelve might lead you.

Keep in mind that sometimes opposites, even in a marriage, do attract. And so some songwriters will purposely choose lyrics that oppose a melody to create a tension or to make a point. "Somebody Got Murdered" by the Clash is a case in point (from *Sandanista*). The words detail a murder and the fact that "somebody's dead forever." Yet the melody is bouncy and jubilant, pointing to the smiling, everyday way that murders are reported on our evening newscasts. Similarly, Paul Simon's "Mother and Child Reunion" is essentially about death, and yet the reggae rhythm and major key tonality of the song emphasize the idea of rebirth and beginning more than death and finality. So in certain cases, when executed carefully, a marriage between words and music in which both parties actually oppose rather than match can be effective.

Walter Becker, formerly of Steely Dan, explained that their music was especially refined and polished to mask the often caustic and acerbic subjects in the lyrics: "The Steely Dan stuff that I used to be involved with we tried to make as slick as we possibly could, because some of the other elements were so subversive that they needed to be sugarcoated or disguised."

A song such as "Everyone's Gone to the Movies," for example, (from *Katy Lied*), concerns itself with a pornographer and yet the music is so pleasing in its catchy jazz-rock structure that many listeners may miss the insidious undertones of the lyrics.

There are few artforms where it is possible to mask or alter one message with another. Randy Newman's song "Sail Away" has one of the most stunning melodies he's ever written. Yet the song is written as an appeal from a white slave-trader to lure potential African slaves to the New World: "Climb aboard, little wog, and sail away with me . . ." Newman's music is as seductive as the slave-trader's promise, underscoring the untrustworthiness of the narrator. "In America you'll get food to eat/Won't have to run in the jungle and scuff up your feet/You'll just sing about Jesus and drink wine all day/It's great to be an American." Music can be used both to reinforce the theme of a song as well as to provide a counterpoint to that theme.

Writing music to words

When composing a tune for a finished lyric, you have to be sensitive to the music that the words already possess. Even without an actual melody, all lyrics have a meter and a tone already uniquely their own. You want the music you write for those words to reflect and support the words. If the lyric bends in a funny way, the melody should also bend. Where the words are forceful, the music should be forceful, and so on.

In other words, you don't want to impose your music onto the words anymore than the words should impose themselves onto the music. Unless your purpose is to create a deliberate contrast between the words and music you want it to seem not only that the words and the music were created by one person, but also that the words and the music were created simultaneously.

Paul Simon said that the words and the music for the title phrase of "Bridge Over Troubled Water" came to him in one flash. Carole King said the same thing about "You've Got a Friend"—that the words and music appeared fullblown, hand in hand. We're not all lucky enough to have these flashes of genius, but it is this effect that we're striving to achieve. An ideal marriage between words and music is one in which it seems as if the music and the words were born at the very same time, like twins, so that their connection couldn't be closer. It's marriage in which you can't imagine a different partner for either and in which there is a sense of inevitability within their union.

Inspiration, Motivation, and Concentration

▼ *How do I avoid writer's block?*

If you're asking this question, you might already have a problem. The best way to avoid what is known as "writer's block" is not to worry about it. The more concentration you put on your inability to write will only make it harder to do so. This condition is the result of anxiety, and anxiety is the antithesis of creativity.

The greatest songs are often created out of joy, out of a recognition that creativity is the highest expression of your soul. Worrying about a "block" will interrupt the creative process and will prohibit your natural creativity from bubbling to the surface. As Carole King said in *SongTalk*, "If nothing is coming, get up and do something else. Then come back again in a relaxed manner. *Trust* that it will be there. If it ever was once, it will be back."

Other writers offer different advice. Randy Newman, who is not noted for being a prolific writer, admitted that when the ideas aren't flowing, it's easy to get negative. "It's pretty awful when nothing is going on. Lots of bad thoughts go

through your mind. Like, 'I'll never do this anymore. Maybe I've gone bad as a person.' " But while Randy does entertain these potentially detrimental thoughts, he counteracts them not by leaving the piano, as does Carole King, but by staying there. His feeling is that if the ideas aren't flowing immediately, you shouldn't give up too soon. "Write something down. Do something. And stay there. Stay there four hours, three hours . . . And good things will happen."

One of the main reasons that people get blocked is that they expect genius to come spilling out onto the page immediately, and when that fails to occur, they get impatient with the process. But a writer must be willing to take chances, to stretch and to fail. As Randy said, "Don't let the critic become bigger than the creator. Don't let it strangle you." And this is imperative to get the flow going. You must suspend that inner voice that says, "No, that's a dumb line, that's a cliché, you've used that before, that sounds stupid," and get on to doing it. By getting ideas down on paper, or recorded on tape, you've got a start, a way into the song. And that's the hardest part: getting going. Once you've started, you have a direction, you have the beginnings of a structure, and you have that creative spark that can be turned into a major fire as long as it isn't extinguished before it has the chance to spread. Get out of your own way and let the song lead you. See where it wants to go and don't be afraid to follow it.

As Rickie Lee Jones told us. "It's been hard for me not to critique my work while I'm doing it. And that can destroy it. 'Cause it really is a spirit being born; it's a living spirit. When people hear it, a spirit happens to them. And you have to be real quiet and careful with it when it's first being born or it can die.... You mustn't interfere with the spirit that's writing."

As Paul Simon wrote in his song "Song About the Moon" (from *Hearts and Bones*), which is essentially a song about how to write songs, "If you want to write a song about the moon, if you want to write a spiritual tune, then *do it*, write a song about the moon." Of course, on the same album Simon has not one but *two* songs called "Think Too Much," emphasizing the reverse of his advice for songwriters, that easy trap into which all of us can fall, thinking too much about what we want to do rather than doing it. The source of all great songs is not only that original inspiration but also the execution of that idea; creating a song out of what is only a thought.

▼ Lately I've been getting nowhere with my songwriting. I can't seem to come up with any good ideas. What should I do?

There are many different things that might be getting in your way. Here's a list of pointers:

1. Time. Give yourself enough of it. If you sit down to write and you don't initially come up with any great ideas, don't abandon the whole ship. It's easy to give up on writing but much tougher to persist. Often it might take an hour simply to get into the frame of mind where you are capable of generating something worthwhile. It is not something that can be forced, and I'm not suggesting forcing it. It is something for which you need to warm up, like any other exercise that requires stamina. Giving yourself the time required to get in touch with your feelings and get beyond the distractions of everyday life is necessary.

2. Environment. What kind of writing environment do you have? Is it relatively clear of clutter, or are you attempting to rise above the mundane trappings of your everyday existence while sitting in the middle of a mountain of unpaid bills, unanswered letters, and other assorted paperwork? I find that it makes a huge difference, when attempting to clear my mind and generate ideas for a song, if my environment is fairly clean and orderly. It it's not, my ability to concentrate and look beyond the ordinary toward the extraordinary is diminished. Your immediate environment reflects your own state of mind. I find that even if my desk is completely clear, I still have trouble getting anywhere if my drawers are snarled with junk. When everything is in a fairly orderly state, it's much easier to tune out the immediate surroundings and concentrate on a song.

3. Play. Do you enjoy songwriting? Is it fun for you? I feel that it's important to remember that nobody *works* music, they *play* music. Music is a gift given to mankind, and if you have the talent to write songs, you have been given the ability to share that gift. When writing, try not to get wrapped up in worry about what is going on. Enjoy the process. Appreciate your prowess in combining words and music. Have fun. Music is meant for enjoyment—you're not laying bricks or building prosthetics, you're making music. And if you don't enjoy the process of creating it, how can it be enjoyable for others? If you have fun while you are doing it and understand that you have a talent and an ability that most people don't possess, it can free you up creatively to write your most vibrant and electric songs. Again, get out of your own way. Let your natural creativity surface and don't submerge it with worry. Think of the way that children will spontaneously create and sing songs, with no worry about if they will sell or get airplay. They create out of the sheer joy of creation, which is the appreciation of being alive.

▼ Should I be writing songs every day?

If you are at liberty to work on songs every day, by all means do it. Many writers do not have this freedom. Since songwriting is an art in which unconscious creation often brings forth the strongest material, condition your mind to be always working on songs. If there are too many gaps between your writing sessions, then you will have to get warmed up each time, not unlike an athlete who must be conditioned. It can take some time to get the ideas flowing, and if you only work on songs for one hour a week, say, that entire hour might be used simply warming up to the point where you are ready to create something new. And when you return next week, you will start the process over.

But by being conditioned, by being in good creative shape, that warm-up will not last as long before you will be able to get the ideas flowing. By writing every day, or as often as possible, you will keep your batteries charged so that when you need a little juice, it will be there.

This is not to imply that it's easy work. It's not. It takes a tremendous amount of energy and determination to stay with something, to see it through, and to not abandon it. Few things are simpler than throwing away undeveloped ideas. The tough part is sticking with them and allowing them to naturally evolve, to gently guide them toward completion. And with anything, the more you do it the better you get at it.

Again, this means suspending that inner critic and being open to writing bad songs. Gerry Goffin told us that he and Carole King wrote hundreds of bad songs before they wrote their first hit, "Will You Love Me Tomorrow?" But that writing enabled them to get into condition, and to exercise those muscles necessary to writing good songs. No baseball player ever hit any homeruns without striking out a number of times as well. The same goes for songwriting. Don't abandon those strange ideas too quickly! Develop them. Even if the song ultimately becomes one you want to keep in your drawer, the act of taking that seed to fruition will get you in good shape for the next one that comes, and the one after that. And that song may be the one on which you establish an entire career.

▼ *When writing a song, do you have to be consciously aware of where you are going with it?*

Well, not really. Since songwriting is an artform in which the strongest songs are often written almost automatically, with the words and the music emerging simultaneously, I wouldn't suggest that completely conscious creation is the only route to take. Too many of our greatest songwriters have admitted that their most powerful songs seemed to have come through them, with little conscious guidance on their part. John Lennon said, "To be creative is to receive a gift. The real music comes to me, the music of the spheres, the music that surpasses understanding, that has not to do with me, that I'm just a channel ... So for that to come through, which is the only joy for me out of the music, is for it to be given to me and for me to transcribe it like a medium." Bob Dylan echoes this sentiment when he said his songs were already written and he just wrote them down.

It's a question I've asked almost every songwriter I've interviewed. Where do you think these ideas for songs come from? Do they come from you or from beyond you? Here's a sampling from *SongTalk* interviews:

Roger McGuinn, formerly of the Byrds: "Songwriting is a spiritual thing. I think it comes from out there."

Felix Cavaliere, formerly of the Rascals: "Some of us are tuners to this vibration that comes through us."

Lamont Dozier, of Holland, Dozier & Holland: "I'm only human and these [songs] are the makings of God. Everything I do that's good, at least, is a reflection of his hand."

Rickie Lee Jones: "I really think there's no doubt that music is dealing with alchemy and magic things. It does things that speak to us in ways that are like a living, other-world thing. I can't explain it and my words are going to diminish what it is, but it's really clear to me that it's a higher thing than any singular person. Once in a while, I write one. But most of the time. . . . most of the time I don't write them."

Jon Anderson of Yes: "Writing is letting go and getting in touch with that energy that is out there and fine-tuning your radar system. There's more music in the spheres than you can imagine."

Eliza Gilkyson: "I feel that [my songs] are prewritten. All I'm doing is transcribing them."

Judy Collins: "Everybody's a channeler. We don't do it. It comes through us. It's not ours."

Gerry Goffin: "Carole [King] always says that

songs come from God. I'm not that pretentious to think God's gonna send me a lyric."

Donovan: "Nobody else was writing my songs. They come from within."

Exene Cervenka of X: "Sometimes you have to be a little metaphysical because people come up to you and say, 'God, how can you do that?' People don't want to take credit because they can't explain it. They don't see how they could be that good at songwriting that they could win Grammys, so they always thank God at the Grammys."

Ray Evans of Livingston & Evans: "You mean like something spiritual? I don't think so. Our ideas came to us because they were assigned."

While I do believe there is a source of music and information that an artist can tap into, unless your personal instrument is well tuned and in good shape, transforming that information into an actual *song* is difficult. I feel that the best approach to songwriting is a mixture of conscious and unconscious creation.

It's like the myth of the aeolian harp that hangs in a tree and makes magnificent music as the wind blows through it. The wind alone cannot create the music nor can the harp. But when the wind blows through a magnificent instrument like the harp, the music is transcendent. Similarly, the songwriter is the instrument through which this source—call it a muse, God, inspiration, whatever you like—comes through. The songwriter has to be in good shape creatively to take that source and translate it into a song. As Robin Williams said, some of us have a direct line to that source while others are on call-waiting.

Being in good shape creatively means being knowledgeable of all the tools at hand—the song structure, use of melody, use of rhyme, use of rhythm, etc.—and being adept enough at your instrument to express that music in this dimension. So while a song can be said to come from beyond, it must come *through* something, and that something is the songwriter. Unless the songwriter has the strength, endurance, and ability to rise to the level of the occasion and face that source head-on, the song will never come into its own.

This is why it's wise for a songwriter to learn all the tools of the trade. Listen to as many songs as you can, study their structure, study melodies,

study lyrics and poetry, learn to be as proficient as possible on your instruments. Then, when the time comes to write, tune out all of that intellectual knowledge and let your instincts take over. Let your creativity flow. Write down or tape all your ideas and don't hinder them by judging if they're good or not. Simply allow yourself to create, and allow yourself to write whatever comes out. Even if it doesn't make sense, or it sounds initially strange, don't get in the way. Listen to your unconscious and see what it is that it's telling you. Enjoy your ability to create music and words, and to combine them.

Then, after that process is complete, go back and see or listen to what you have done. At this stage, you can bring back all the faculties you tuned out earlier, and intellectually analyze your work and see if it adds up. In this way, you combine the earlier unconscious approach—in which you let the elements fly and land where they may—with this conscious attempt to control and order the elements. At this stage you might be surprised by the connections between what originally seemed to be disparate matters. These unconscious connections that we make unknowingly can be quite powerful in songs, connecting images and meanings like the logic of dreams. And as songs are listened to on both unconscious and conscious levels (active and passive listening), it makes sense to approach them on both levels.

▼ Are there any ways of consciously getting in touch with that unconscious source, such as using drugs?

While it would be foolish to deny that at times drugs or alcohol might have enabled certain songwriters to connect with parts of their own psyche that they might not connect with otherwise, as a general rule it's best to steer clear of the use of any controlled substances to inspire your writing. Drugs or drink, like any agent, will take you out of your reality for a while and give you a different perspective. It's so easy to get wrapped up in the distractions of everyday life that this might seem like an easy way out. But if you do anything that shifts your perspective on a regular basis, you adopt a new perspective, and one that might be even more distant from that inner source that you are trying to embrace. Anything that shifts your perspective too frequently will soon create a new "reality" and that will become the only perspective through which you can view the world. If you're always high, then your "normal" consciousness will cease to be normal.

Songwriting takes a lot of energy, and anything you do to yourself that depletes that source of energy will be detrimental to your writing. And while a drug like cocaine, for example, might seem to give you more energy initially, it will soon require all your energy just to keep getting more, and to satisfy your need for the drug. The world needs no more intelligent and talented musicians reduced to living like junkies, worrying about where the next fix will come from rather than putting that energy into writing and recording songs. Beware! It's a dead-end.

Besides, you can take far healthier paths to reach those inner sources.

▼ Is daily exercise beneficial for songwriters?

Yes. Unless your body is in good shape, I don't think your mind can be. And it takes a lot of energy and stamina simply to *stay there* and keep working on an idea, even when it seems as if it's going nowhere. Staying physically in shape means that you will have the energy to stay in one place and concentrate. If you don't exercise, your circulation will be poor and this results in a general sluggishness and malaise.

Some songwriters have suggested that too much exercise will actually drain you, and not leave you with the vigor necessary to generate good songs. You have to decide what is best for you by getting in touch with your own metabolism. If you're the kind of person for whom exercise seems to drain your creative abilities, work out a schedule where you can exercise after your writing session. This might be a great release for the tension you build up hunched over a piano, guitar, or desk. Find what works best for you, but try to find a way to exercise daily. It's said that twenty minutes of aerobic exercise on a daily basis is the minimum exercise required for an adult. And aerobic exercise refers to physical exercise that gets our hearts pumping: a leisurely walk does not quality (of

course, it's better than nothing!). But if you can get in only twenty minutes of aerobic exercise—be it running, swimming, cycling, whatever—it's likely that you will find yourself thinking more clearly and easily.

Songwriters are like windows through which the light of inspiration can shine. But if that window is dirty, that light won't be able to shine through. And if that window is only partially cleaned, but obscured slightly by some substance, then that light will be fractured and unclear. A songwriter should strive to make sure that window is clean and clear in every way, and in doing so they will enable that light of inspiration to come through completely in all its magnificence.

▼ I've only written two songs in my life but I think they're both commercial enough to make a lot of money. Are two songs enough to get started?

It depends what you are trying to accomplish with your two songs. Do you want to make money or do you want to be a songwriter?

It's important for a songwriter to understand his reasons for writing songs. If your main purpose is to make money, there are many easier ways of going about that than trying to write songs. That's not to say that people haven't made millions by writing songs. But many of those songs were written not to make money but out of the need to write them, that feeling that you have no choice. If you are writing songs out of love, or out of the need for authentic artistic expression, your songs will have the power of authenticity; they will be real.

Why? Because if your purpose in writing has more to do with commerce than art, then you have to pay more attention to that which is outside of you than that which is within: you have to listen to the radio and consciously attempt to mimic whatever trend is currently in vogue. You have to figure out what the kids (not the adults, since kids make up the majority of the record-buying public) are listening to and try to write something like that. And in music, all trends eventually pass and anything written to match a trend will quickly seem dated. Paying more attention to the marketplace than to the voice within you—the true source of creativity—can only result in the creation of a work that is derivative and ultimately empty.

Whereas the opposite—writing that which is true to you regardless of what's currently on the charts—will result in personal, potentially timeless songs; songs that apply to our lives no matter what year it might be.

Many songwriters agree with this contention, though not all of them do. Pete Seeger told *Song-Talk* that he agreed with Woody Guthrie's feeling that anytime you write songs to make money you are killing yourself artistically. The talent to write a song is a true gift, an ability to connect with your deepest feelings and express them with words and music so that others can both understand and feel those same emotions. To use that gift only to make money can make it difficult in the future to use that gift for any other purpose. You might find, when wanting to write a song of expression, that you can no longer connect with your own voice since you turned elsewhere for that source.

This is not to imply that there's anything wrong with making money writing songs, quite to the contrary. But if making money is your only motivation, you might lose the primary joy of writing songs, whatever it was that inspired you to write one in the first place. This is the danger all songwriters face when songwriting becomes a profession and not simply a means of expression. Rickie Lee Jones told us how songwriting lost its joy for her when it became her job, and it took her some time to remember the feeling of doing it just for fun. It's important to stay in touch with the inherent joy of music to create something that will last.

Frank Zappa, who has never written what can be called a truly commercial song (although he has had his fluke hits), disagrees completely with this idea. He said this to *SongTalk*: "Any songwriter who had to choose between being rich and timeless, if he chose timeless, he's probably out of a job. . . . Unless there is a massive change of attitude at the distribution level, there is little hope that anyone who is doing anything other than formula swill will have an opportunity to have his music recorded, let alone transmitted." What he says is not false: chances of getting a song published are greater if that song is similar to something on the radio *right now*. A "formula" song might have a better chance at commercial success than a song that stretches the boundaries. There are numerous examples of songs that became hits because they repeated a successful formula at the right time. Is this plagiarism? Do you want to be involved? You have to figure out for yourself what your motivations are for writing songs and what you ultimately want to accomplish. If you want to get a few cuts on albums, you will get a better reaction from publishers if your songs aren't too unusual. If, however, you want to write songs that are entirely new, that say things that have never been said before, you'll have a harder time getting published. But you will have the satisfaction of knowing that you stayed true to your artistic vision and that art, and not commerce, is what rules your life.

"Yeah, but get real," you might say. "I want to write artistic songs but I have to make a living." Todd Rundgren, another songwriter who has had a few hits but who mostly writes uncommercial, unusual, and artistic songs, gave *SongTalk* this answer to that statement: "I would say don't attempt to make a living and consider yourself an artist at the same time. If someone wants to be an artist, then get a job that pays and you can depend on and don't be any less devoted to your artistry. . . . You've got to decide, 'If I'm going to be a songwriter, I'm going to have to devote myself to that craft and not try to depend on making a living on it.' Because if you depend on making a living on it, you have to do one of two things: you have to go out, find a connection, schmooze them, or you have to consciously prostitute yourself and write whatever is the currently acceptable style of music."

Joan Baez reiterated Todd's statement when we asked her how an artist can survive in these disposable times. "Get a day job," she answered.

Songwriters vs. singer-songwriters

It's important here to draw the distinction between those songwriters writing songs for others, and those who are writing for themselves. This distinction is sometimes referred to as being a "vertical" or a "horizontal" writer: the "vertical" writer writes songs and performs them herself; the "horizontal" writer writes songs only for others to perform.

If you are a "vertical" artist, you can have more freedom in your writing since you can write songs for your own particular voice and style. A "horizontal" songwriter has to write commercially viable songs or he will have no chance of getting songs published or recorded; your songs have to be judged by music publishers for whom music is a business, not an art. Publishers are not interested in contributing to the art of humanity nor do they care much about the creation of a timeless song. (Even though a song that can be recorded for years to come will ultimately be more successful than one that only fits the trends of a particular year or month. Try convincing a publisher of this, though.) If a song is similar to something currently successful, chances are that they will respond to it.

However, if you are a "vertical" artist, writing for yourself or your band, you already have someone to perform the songs and you can get away with being more artistic and paying less (or no) attention to current trends. And as a "vertical" artist you will have to deal with record companies rather than music publishers, who have shown the willingness to invest in artists that have a unique artistic vision.

(An exception is the "horizontal" writer who teams up with a singer or band. If you can find an artist or band to perform your material, you will have a voice and some say as to how a song is produced. If the artist or band gets a record contract, you will be able to have your songs recorded without the consent of a publisher, a fortunate position to be in.)

Tracy Chapman's song "Fast Car" was a major radio hit for her. If however, she brought that song to a music publisher she would have little to no chance of getting it recorded by another artist. Why? Because there was nothing on the radio even remotely like it at the time. A publisher might hear it and say, "Well, the hook's kind of weak and the whole song is kind of depressing. Got anything a little more upbeat?" But her record company was willing to take a chance on the song, wisely, and when people heard it they were refreshed by the unusual occurrence of hearing a personal, artistic song on the radio. So Tracy Chapman, being a "vertical" artist, was able to have success with an artistic and unusual song, and stretched the boundaries of what is acceptable for Top 40 radio.

So, it's important for songwriters to be aware of their motivations for writing songs. If you are writing songs for others to sing, you will have to provide publishers with potential radio hits. I've had many experiences of sitting at a publisher's desk, listening with him to one of my tapes, and hearing him say, "I love these songs. These are great! Can't do anything with them, but I love them!"

There have been many instances of great artistic songs becoming hits. But most of them are written by the artists who perform them. There are countless instances of this: the songs of the Beatles, for example, never regurgitated something that had already been successful. They didn't even seek to repeat their own formulas for success, choosing instead to constantly progress artistically. Since they were the Beatles, however, the public was willing to follow them into new areas. Paul Simon, too, has had hits with some very unusual songs. Who before him had a song called "Kodachrome"? Yet he made it work.

But songs written by writers for other artists are often safe songs that conform without challenging too much, the exception being songs that catch on precisely because of their unique qualities. Songs such as "Bette Davis Eyes" (written by Jackie DeShannon and recorded by Kim Carnes) and "Walk Like an Egyptian" (written by Liam Sternberg and recorded by the Bangles) are examples of this—unusual songs that became hits because they were both commercial and unique: they each had something new to say and yet did it in a way that was acceptable for radio play. But this is rare.

If you are a songwriter planning to write for other singers, you'll find that once you get your foot in the door, you'll have a better time getting songs recorded. Once you have some kind of a track record, publishers will take you seriously and be more open to your more adventurous songs. But to get to that place will take one song that they can take a chance on before even knowing you. Something that sounds similar to other things they know will have a better chance. An artistically adventurous song might have a chance if it sounds commercial enough to fit into the current major radio format.

Sometimes an inventive and even revolutionary lyric becomes accepted as a hit because it is couched in seductive music. Almost any song by Steely Dan is a good example of this as we have already seen in the example of "Everyone's Gone to the Movies." The lyrics are never empty or vacuous; there's always something interesting—maybe even unscrupulous—going on, yet the music that contains it is always smooth and slick and shiny as a new car. The listener gets hooked in on the music, often without even comprehending the message of the song.

Whichever kind of song you write, the best thing to do is write as much as you can, and develop your songs based on your musical and artistic instincts. Then, when the time comes to think about marketing your songs, put on your business hat and look at your songs differently, not as the writer but as a potential publisher. Which songs have you written that would be the best to present to a publisher? When you have decided, make good demos of those songs, using them as the means to get started. And once you have gotten a few of your songs published, you might have an opportunity to place some of the more unusual ones.

▼ Isn't it important for songwriters to listen to the radio and pay attention to trends?

There's nothing wrong with listening to the radio if you do so for enjoyment or simply to stay abreast of new songs and artists. But to listen so you can follow or mimic a current trend will do you no good. For one thing, most trends pass quickly; by the time you get a song published and recorded, it's likely that the trend you were following has already gone. The songwriters who don't follow the trends but set them are always going to be the ones in the forefront. You have the choice of being a follower or a leader.

As an example, for many years a techno-pop sound featuring mostly synthesizers and drum machines was prevalent. Along comes Tracy Chapman with an acoustic guitar at the heart of her music, and people loved it precisely because at that moment it seemed unusual, it went against the trend. So anytime you see a musical trend develop-

ing, you are wiser to ignore it altogether than attempt to get on the bandwagon.

Another danger in listening to the radio is that you might unwillingly steal someone's idea, that easy trap of plagiarism we mentioned earlier. Tom Waits has compared writing songs to those carnival games where you move the miniature crane and try to pick up a prize. You might go for a diamond ring and end up with some fuzzy dice. Songwriting is the same way: you don't always end up with what you aimed for. For this reason, you have to be careful about what you listen to. Everything you hear becomes grist for the mill; whatever goes in is bound to come out.

When I get particularly enamored of a certain song, I'll listen to it constantly and sing it to myself to the point of learning it as well as one of my own. At this point I often find myself coming up with melodic or rhythmic ideas that seem wonderfully new, only to realize a few moments later that I've ripped off that song I've been singing for weeks. A songwriter has to be careful about this.

▼ Most of my songs are longer than average radio songs. Is this okay?

No. If you want your songs to be published, they do have to fit certain time limitations. While a few long songs have become hits ("Hey Jude" by the Beatles and "American Pie" by Don McClean are examples), these are mostly exceptions. For the most part, publishers are looking for songs that are no longer than about three minutes.

If you are a vertical artist with no intention of having your songs covered by other singers, you can write longer, extended songs for yourself. Both Bob Dylan and Joni Mitchell have written extended songs that are undisputable masterpieces. Again, there are no rules.

But to get a publisher interested, brevity is important. And there are aesthetic reasons as well for the use of brevity. As Pete Seeger once said, "Any damn fool can be complicated but it takes genius to attain simplicity." It's true: if you can make a song complete in three verses it will be more powerful than a song that takes eleven verses to make its point.

An example of masterful use of brevity in a song is Randy Newman's song "In Germany Before the War." It's only three minutes and thirty-nine seconds long and yet it has more going on in it than 90 percent of the songs you hear on the radio. There are characters—the old man and the young girl; there is a sense of place: Dusseldorf, Germany; there is a specific sense of time: 1934. And there is conflict, created both by the words and the artful use of dissonance.

Another fine example of a masterful use of brevity in a song is from an older work, the standard "My Funny Valentine" written in 1937 by Rodgers and Hart. (To hear a breathtaking interpretation of this song, check out Rickie Lee Jones' *Girl at Her Volcano*).

The entire song is only thirty-six measures long with no repeats, and yet a whole world is created in this short span of time; it's a love song in which the object of this love is not romanticized: "Your looks are laughable/unphotographable, Yet you're my favorite work of art. . . ." This contrast is carried through the song; it's a valentine that possesses more humor than beauty. Yet the power of love proves stronger than any of these trivialities, emphasized by the simple yet beautiful C-minor melody: "But don't change a hair for me, not if you care for me, stay, little valentine, stay! Each day is Valentine's day." It's a perfect song. It's no longer than it need be: the lyrical idea is fleshed out, establishing a love that rises above all imperfections, and the music that matches these sentiments is simple yet moving; it rises and falls with the arc of the lyrics and finally ends up resolved on an E-flat major chord, moving us from the minor into a major key for a sense of finality.

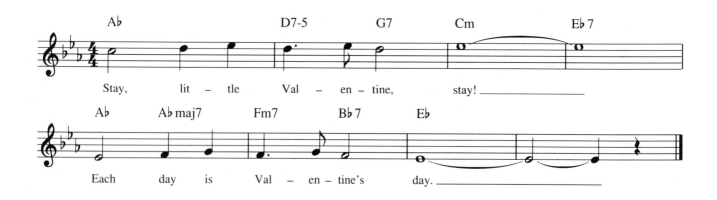

7

Rewriting

▼ *When I finish a song, I hate to go back and rewrite it at all. Is rewriting songs important?*

Yes. Most beginning songwriters consider it an accomplishment simply to finish a song. And it is an accomplishment, but as time goes on you must be concerned more with quality than quantity. This is a lesson I've learned well, having written as many songs as possible when I began. Having another one finished and under my belt was my goal, and at that time, the quality of the song was secondary. After a while, however, I came to the realization that not all of those songs were really keepers, and that when the time came to record or perform any of them, there were only a handful—maybe four—that I would deem worthy.

So I did what any good songwriter must do. I began to rework and rewrite my songs. After finishing one (actually a *draft* of one), I would go back and see if there were any parts of the song that were weak and that didn't excite me. I would analyze the lyrics, making sure that there wasn't a single line that bothered me in any way. I would also analyze the melody in the same way. And a truly good songwriter will replace the weak parts with newer parts that are even stronger, adding power to the overall structure of the song.

It is said that any attempt to achieve perfection is godly. As a songwriter, you are attempting to create a perfect being. And while no song, or person, ever achieves complete perfection, some come closer than others. As songwriters, we work to make each song we write as perfect as possible.

While being prolific is admirable, it is quality and not quantity which will matter in the long run. The work of Randy Newman is a great example of this. Rather than churn out new products every year, he waits until he has a new collection of songs that will equal or surpass his previous work. Because of this, he has the reputation of being one of the great masters of the song. His personal standard is extremely high and to reach it takes time, patience, and some frustration.

Ultimately you will come to the understanding that it only takes one great song to start a career. And while some great songs are created spontaneously, with no rewriting at all, most songs are based on what is essentially a rough draft; the songwriter follows his inspiration as far as it will take him, being careful not to get in the way. And when that process is finished, the writer must go back and examine those ideas to determine what works and what doesn't work. This is the craft stage of songwriting, and every good songwriter must be a good craftsman, able to take a roughly formed piece of clay and mold a song out of it.

▼ *Maybe my standards aren't that high, but I'm usually satisfied with my songs as soon as they're done. What kind of things do you attempt to change?*

As time goes on and you write more and more songs, you will see that certain songs you have written possess a magical nature, a transcendence, if you will, while others remain commonplace. Sometimes that greatness is given to you. Other times, though, you get only a little piece of it, and to make the song appear seamless around it takes a lot of hard work.

Analyze the songs that don't move you and about which you are not as proud. What is it about them, in your mind, that you don't like? Here's a checklist just for starters.

Does your new song have:

A strong, memorable melody?

An interesting and pleasing rhythm?

A sound structure with a rich chorus?

A good contrast between the verses and chorus?

A good title?

A building of tension and eventual release?

Understandable lyrics, not just by you but by the world at large?

Original lyrics without clichés?

A strong rhyme scheme?

Sonorous, flowing word choices?

This is only a beginning of considerations. It's up to you to decide what works and what doesn't in a song. Use this checklist and add other qualities to it that you think either make or break a song.

▼ *How do you go about rewriting a melody?*

After completing a draft of the song, pay attention first to the melody. Perhaps the best test of a melody is to sing it without any instrument. Burt Bacharach, one of the great melodists of our time, said that this is the very method he uses. "If you can hum or whistle a tune without playing an instrument, and it sounds good, you know you have something there."

I've looked back at songs I've written in which I liked the lyrics but realized I had settled on a monochromatic melody with very little range. Writing music based more on chord changes than melody can create this. In some songs I found there was an impressive barrage of chord changes but a melody that was rather stagnant. It's important to remember that it's the melody, not the changes,

that people are going to react to. The majority of people hear melodies instinctually; they've been doing it their whole lives. It's only a small percentage of the population—that minority known as musicians—who would ever remark, "Hey, great chord progression! Love the way that B-flat-minor-13th goes to the D-minor-ninth." You can have chords running up to the sky and it won't matter at all if the melody isn't moving as well.

One way to do this is to be aware of the range of your melody. After finishing a song, go back and analyze exactly how many notes you have used and notice the range between the lowest and the highest notes. Is it large? Have you utilized even a whole octave? It can be surprising sometimes to see how small of a range of notes are used, sometimes no bigger than a fifth. If the range is too small, go back and work on it. Change the chords if need be, and see where in the melody you can enlarge the range.

▼ ———————————

Much attention has been given to John Lennon and his lyrical influence in the Beatles on Paul McCartney. But little is ever said about McCartney's huge *melodic* influence on Lennon. Often John would bring in a song and Paul would say something like, "How about going to a different note there? You've already used that note many times." This influence encouraged Lennon, no doubt, to be as inventive with his melodies as he was with his lyrics. Would he have written songs as beautiful as "Julia" and "Imagine" later in his career without McCartney's early influence? From the very start, Paul was musically adventurous; even an early song like "I Want to Hold Your Hand" was polychromatic. It's in the key of C yet arcs in the bridge up a fifth to G minor before returning to tonic for the verse. As McCartney said, "You're in C and it's pretty ordinary. Going to a G minor takes you to a whole new world. It was exciting." Another early Beatles' song "From Me to You" is also in C with a G-minor bridge. Lennon and McCartney may not have known how to read music, but they sure knew what sounded good.

———————————————— ▲

Another ingredient that can make a melody strong is the use of melodic skips. Melodically, a step is the movement from one note to the next consecutive note, from a C to a D, for example, and from a D to an E. A skip is a movement between any two notes that is larger than a step, for example, from C to G.

Jimmy Webb, one of the great melodists of our time, discussed this use of melodic skips: "I started writing with a lot of skips probably because I was under the influence of Burt Bacharach . . . His melodies are very unpredictable and skip in not odd but unusual directions. I think that's the way you get kind of a new melody, a catchy melody, by playing with intervals like that."

The use of melodic skips is extremely effective in the enlarging and enriching of a melody. The famous chorus of "Somewhere over the Rainbow" (music by Harold Arlen; lyrics by E. Y. Harburg) is a perfect example of this, a skip of a full octave is shown at the bottom of this page.

This skip on "somewhere" accentuates the longing of the lyric and the reaching upwards toward the sky. It's a full octave skip, from E flat to E flat, followed on "over the rainbow" by a slight skip down and then three steps back to the E flat. Then, we get another full octave skip downwards ("way") and *another* skip upwards, appropriately, on "up" before a step down to the B flat on the word "high." With only seven of Harburg's words, Arlen employs four major skips! It's why this is one of the world's most beautiful and enduring melodies, every bit as enchanting today as when it was first written to be used in the film version of *The Wizard of Oz* in 1938.

Another effective means of using a melodic skip is when a melody goes up a skip and then down a skip even larger than the first one, so that you end up lower than where you began. An example is Stephen Sondheim's "Send in the Clowns" (written in one night when told that his musical *A Little Night Music* needed an extra song).

The melody starts with short ascending phrases on the questions "Isn't it rich? Are we a pair?" It stays within a small minor third on "Me here at last on the ground . . ." It is then that the melodic skips occur, amplifying the lyric "You in mid-air." The note on "you" is a G, the highest point of the previous phrase. From there the tune skips up a minor third to a B flat ("in") and then down *an entire octave* to a lower B flat ("mid-") before going up a step to the C on "air." It's this ascending skip preceding a large *descending* skip that gives the melody both its breadth and its tone of wistful melancholy. The effect is of a rising and falling; a joy interlaced with sorrow.

▼ How do you go about rewriting lyrics?

Understandable and original lyrics are difficult to create. No one wants their songs to be trite, so we begin by avoiding clichés in lyric writing in favor of something that is original. The danger in doing this, of course, is that you can try so hard to be original that you lose sight of the message of the song. Originality is wonderful but is it comprehensible?

When I was fourteen I had the lucky opportunity to play a song of mine for the late great singer-songwriter, Steve Goodman (the writer of "City of New Orleans" and countless other wonderful songs). I cornered him backstage after a concert

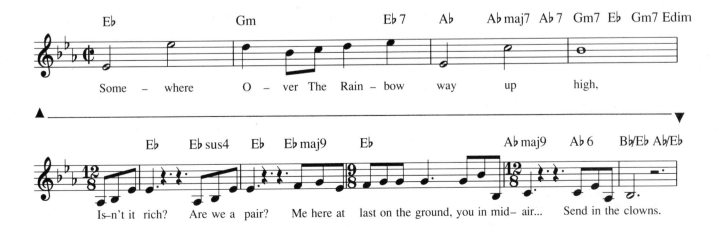

and asked him to listen to a new song of mine. He generously agreed and even allowed me to play it on his big black guitar.

I played the song, which had an abstract, slightly psychedelic lyric. Steve listened to it and politely told me, "Yeah, I understand what you're saying in the song. But I think you could have said all of it in about two lines."

This was a revelation for me! It had an immediate and lasting effect on my writing. No longer did I settle for obfuscation in my lyrics—the idea that if you are poetic and original enough in your lyrics that people will read a message into them. I decided, at that moment, to try to write songs that were more immediately clear and understandable rather than abstract. And this is a good deal harder, because not only must you be entirely aware of what you are trying to say in a song, but you have to do so in a manner that will allow others to understand the song.

This is not to suggest here that you cease being poetic in your work, or that you abandon all abstract ideas that come your way. Only that you should strive to be clear in your writing, sure of what you are saying and how you want to say it. Often a mixture of the abstract and the concrete can be quite effective. And, of course, there are themes and topics that can't be easily dealt with in common language. But by balancing the abstract and concrete elements of your song, you can express yourself more effectively.

As Janis Ian told *SongTalk*, "When you write a verse that is abstract, the chorus better make it clear. And when the chorus is abstract, you need a very basic verse."

Make sure that your lyric is understandable, not just by you but by the world at large. Often people will write songs that they have figured were easily understandable when in fact they employed very personal symbology. If you are going to be abstract in your song, are you using the abstraction for a purpose? Are you sure of its meaning? Or is it present simply because it sounds interesting? These are the questions you ask yourself while in the rewriting stage, while connecting those disparate parts and seeing if they not only connect for you, but in terms of the entire song. Work with those sections that are unsure of themselves until

they feel right. You'll find that fixing one part will strengthen the entire body of a song.

▼ How do I know when the work is done and there's no more need for rewriting?

That's one of those determinations you have to learn to make based on your own judgment. Usually it's a good idea to get away from the song for a day or two so that you can gain some distance from it and hear it anew again. Some writers liken this to hearing it as if you didn't write it so that you can honestly gauge how it affects you.

When you listen to the song after a few days, pay close attention to the lyrics and the music as well as the overall structure. Are there any parts of the song that let you down or bother you in any way? Are there any parts in which the song could have been developed more? If so, you know that your work is not over. But if there are no parts that could use development and it all works well as a whole, you could very well be finished with this one. Only you can say.

Naturally, nothing in art is ever truly perfect. Even Dylan, who has come closer to perfection in songs than most writers ever do, has gone back and vastly rewritten songs that were already brilliantly written in the first place. Like any great artist, he senses that "divine dissatisfaction," that feeling that your art can always come a little closer to godliness. For example, he took his beautiful song "Simple Twist of Fate" (originally from *Blood on the Tracks*) and changed it even to the extent of shifting it from a first-person narrative to a third-person account (on his album *Bob Dylan at Budokan*). If Dylan can do this with a song that's not only been recorded and distributed around the globe, but that has also been universally praised for its greatness, you can surely do it with a song nobody but you has heard yet. It's hard but it's worth it.

Michelangelo, an artist who has surely come close to godliness in all of his work and especially his sculptures, used to approach a block of marble with the feeling that the perfect form was already present inside the unsculptured material. Rather than invent or impose a figure onto the marble, Michelangelo would simply cut away all the excess marble around the figure until it was manifest. In

David were born. In this same way, when you approach a rewrite, don't externally impose your ideas onto the work, but look into your first draft and see what is there. Then set out to trim the excess until the basic, essential, near-perfect figure is present.

Only you can determine when your creation is complete, and to do so you have to tune into that inner voice you worked so hard to ignore during the early stages of creation. As any mother bird knows, if the child is not ready and his wings are not strong enough, it will fall to the ground unable to fly. Like a bird, a song can soar beautifully all on its own if its development has been complete.

Getting Feedback

▼ *When I finish a song, should I bother playing it for my friends and family, even if they don't know anything about music?*

Yes. Creating a song is not unlike building a house from the inside out. You might have a brilliant structure with some truly fabulous rooms, and yet from the outside the house can look ramshackle. It's hard to be objective about your own work and songs are especially hard to judge. Lines that might have special resonance for you might mean nothing to someone else. Similarly, a tune you might find to be beautiful might not work at all for another person. For that reason, it's imperative that you play your songs for whoever will listen to them. And then, and this part may be even harder, *listen* to what people have to say about your songs and learn to respect their opinion.

But why should I listen to my brother, you might say, since he knows nothing about music? A common question, and the answer is because songs are not written only for other musicians. They are written for the public at large, the majority of whom know nothing about music. Yet, as the saying goes, they do know what they like. Chances are you'll learn more about your song from an electrician or a bus driver than you would from a fellow musician. A musician might be so impressed by your unusual chord progressions or strange rhythms that he'd lose sight of the song's overall quality. To the electrician or the bus driver, it doesn't matter what chords are used; if it's a two-chord song, they could still love it because it works, because it's right. And this is the real test of a song. Do people like it? Do they understand it? Are they getting out of it what you wanted them to? Have you expressed yourself successfully? Just as you don't have to be a chef to know what foods you like, you don't have to be a musician to know what songs work for you.

I've played songs for friends of mine who are composers of modern classical music. These guys far prefer some interesting dissonance over a pretty melody. Both of them gravitated toward a song of mine that had a peculiar chord sequence and melody, revolving around diminished chords and deceptive cadences. Musically, I was pretty proud of it because it was hard to play. I thought it was both jazzy and sophisticated. I played the same song for my sister, who has excellent taste in music, and she admitted to me that she hated it. Now neither my sister nor my composer-friends were wrong in any way. Yet I knew she was responding more to the song as a whole than to the bizarre use of chords, and I valued her opinion every bit as much—maybe even more—than my composer-friends. The fact that she's not a musician makes her even more qualified, in my opinion, than they are to judge my songs.

Of course, when playing songs for a friend or family member you have to make sure that your listener is able to be honest with you. If your mother or your aunt are the type who say, "Wow! Another great one! How do you do it?" She probably won't be much help. You need to play your songs for people who aren't afraid to be brutally honest with you. If they tell you honestly when they don't like a song (and why), you can be sure that they are telling the truth when they say they *do* like something. My dad is a writer and so is much more picky about lyrics than music, abhorring anything that is slightly trite. And since he's such an avid reader, more things seem trite to him than to the average listener. This has caused me in my writing to fight hard against any triteness and try my hardest to write original, interesting lyrics. And since he has been so honest about when lyrics don't work for him, I know he's telling the truth when he says he does like something. It's important to have a fairly brutal critic in your life, someone you can count on to never be polite with you about a song. Politeness won't help you as much as honesty when it comes to feedback. So when playing songs for friends and family, make sure you have the kind of relationship that allows them to be frank with you. While it's nice to get support, no matter how putrid a song might be, it's far more helpful for you to have a person in your life who can offer honest, constructive criticism.

What you then do with that criticism is up to you. There are a few choices: you can throw away the song altogether, you can put it away for the time being with the intention of reworking it someday, or you can immediately try to rewrite it, turning its weaknesses into strengths. If you totally disagree with the criticism you receive, you can also choose to ignore it. After all, every opinion is only that—a single opinion. You are the creator in charge and you have the final say. Ultimately, the song has to please you for it to succeed. If a song seems perfect to you and you are unable to change it, that is a valid feeling. Sometimes, though, given a little thought and time, even what seemed to be a perfect song can be open to changes. If you're smart, you can learn a lot by the way people respond to your work. You can discover where you've failed and where you've succeeded.

▼ *How else should I test out my songs?*

One of the best tests of a song is how it sounds without any production, with only one instrument (a piano or a guitar) and a vocal. This reduces the song to its basic form, the words and the music.

Often good production can mask a poor or incomplete song. When people hear your tapes do they respond to the song itself, or do they say things like "Hey, great snare, man! Super drum sound!"? Remember that production does not make a song. Often people make demos of what they consider to be a song, and which is in fact an exciting-sounding musical track that in no way adds up to a song. They'll have a drum track with some synth pads, a bass line and some power guitar chords, and a guitar solo or two thrown in. And they'll say, "See—here's where the chorus goes. All I need is someone to come up with some good words and a melody." Little do they realize that without words and a melody, there is no song. Sure, it's possible to fashion a song from those beginnings. And some writers are quite adept at writing from existing tracks. But understand that tracks of music, no matter how elaborate they might be, do not make a song.

The words and the melody of a song are like the structure of a house. No matter how the house is decorated, the structure stays the same. (Unless, of course, you start knocking down walls and actually change the structure.) Production is essentially decoration, something that is added later to make the house look better. There's no sense in worrying about the decorations before you've built the house. Similarly, any house dependent on decorations to mask its weaknesses (as in, "Don't worry about that hole in the floor; we'll put a couch over it") is a house with an inadequate foundation. Any song that depends on production for it to succeed is an incomplete song. However, if your house looks wonderful even without any furniture (to stretch this analogy even farther), if it looks great based only on the interaction of space and line and works perfectly as an organic whole, you've got a super house with a strong structure that doesn't need much in the way of decoration. There's nothing to hide, only strengths to enhance. Production should emphasize the strengths of a song, not mask the weaknesses.

▼ *Is performing in public a good way to test my songs?*

It can be if you are a good performer. If you're not, your performance could get in the way of people hearing your song. Karla Bonoff told us that the first time she played her song "Someone to Lay Down Beside Me" for Linda Ronstadt, Linda was unimpressed. The reason, according to Karla, was that she was extremely nervous when playing the song and didn't perform it well. Later, Linda Ronstadt heard Karla's friend Kenny Edwards play the song and loved it. She went on to record it and it became one of the biggest hits of her career. (Karla Bonoff has since grown into a wonderful performer.) So you have to ask yourself the question, "Can I do my songs justice?"

If the answer is yes, then performing your own material can be an ideal way to test your songs. Many cities have clubs that hold what are often known as "open stage" or "open mike" nights. These are nights in which anyone can get up on stage and do one or two songs. These are the perfect places both for testing out a song and for honing your performance skills.

Remember, if you are only starting out at performing in public, don't get in the way of the song. Just as you don't want to get in the way of the song when writing it, the same goes when performing it. If you worry too much about how you are going over as a performer, you can hinder your ability to put across the song. Get in touch with what moved you to write the song in the first place, and let that spirit come across. Sing the words clearly so that they can be understood; you want people to have a chance to hear the words. Let the song guide you.

▼ *Do these showcases pay?*

No. But unless music is something you are willing to do for free, chances are you won't ever make much money doing it. To succeed you have to be willing to do it for love and not money. And the truth of the matter is that in most big cities, there are so many songwriters competing to be heard that unless you perform for free you might have no chance of being heard. In Los Angeles, for example, there are so many songwriters and so many bands struggling to get their feet in the door, that club owners take advantage of this glut of available talent and pay solo acts and bands little to nothing.

▼ ─────────────────────────

Some clubs will pay a band a percentage of the "door" (however much the club took in on cover charges) and others will give the band the entire "door." Many clubs are set up in a way that you only receive a portion of the door after a required number of paying people come in to see you. How much you earn becomes entirely dependent on how many people you get to come out and see you.

Still other clubs have another setup that can be good or bad, depending on what kind of a following you have. They will sell you—the act—a certain number of tickets for slightly less than the door value of the tickets, which you have to sell yourself. If you can sell enough of these you can earn a profit, but if you can't sell them you can take a great loss.

In many cases, bands or artists will rent a club or a hall and present their own showcase. Again, the act is completely responsible for how much they make, based on how big of a draw they have.

───────────────────────── ▲

There are countless songwriters willing to invest their own money to have a chance to perform and to receive exposure. When you get into hiring musicians, we are talking about a greater expense. So not only might you not earn any money performing, you can lose a great deal.

Is it worth it? It depends on you. If you're not a performer, then certainly none of this relates to you. You will have to find other artists to perform your material. If you are a performer of your own songs, though, you must be willing to invest whatever it takes to succeed. Those performers who earned nothing for years or lost money and didn't give up eventually rise to the top and become successful. Bruce Hornsby, for example, spent seven years sending tapes to record companies and being rejected before he finally got a record deal and started a career. It was his persistence, his refusal to lose faith in vision and his ability that eventually allowed him to be the success he is today.

▼ ───────────────────────────

The story of Bruce Hornsby's persistance and eventual rise to fame is a good one for any songwriter to know. For seven years straight he sent his tapes to the same ten record companies and for seven years he was turned down.

The tapes that Hornsby would send contained his original songs, some of which, like "The Way It Is," went on to become major radio hits. But one of the key components of that song was the unprecedented use of a jazzy acoustic piano in a pop setting. It was a sound Hornsby didn't use at first because he thought it would scare off record companies. This was during the time when synthesizers were in vogue and nothing else then on radio used any acoustic piano. For this reason Bruce would record all his songs with synths instead of piano to fit in: "I was writing these songs on piano," he told us, "and I'd always transfer them to synthesizers . . . And I'd come away thinking, 'Damn. I thought these songs were better than this. It sure feels better to me when I play them on piano.' " This dissatisfaction went on for seven years, until Hornsby took a risk and recorded what he called a "secret tape" featuring his piano sound. He sent the tape only to Windham Hill, figuring that only a "new age" record company would consider this music that followed no trends. The tape was leaked to the major record companies and they loved it. "I guess I was a slow learner because it took me a long time to get to this *basic realization* to just go back to what I do naturally. After being passed on seventy times—seven years and ten labels—finally this was the tape that didn't get passed on."

The lesson here is to do what you do best, regardless of trends. Not only did Hornsby get a record contract, his songs went on to be major hits and others have begun to imitate his piano sounds on their records and demos. It's a tale of persistence and vision: through seven years of rejection, Hornsby persevered and finally achieved success by being himself and doing that which he had been doing from the start.

As Van Dyke Parks said, "It doesn't make sense trying to be successful doing what other people are doing." Trust your instincts and be yourself. Nobody else can write your songs but you.

───────────────────────────── ▲

▼ *I know I'm already a good songwriter. Is there any reason I should go to a songwriter's workshop?*

Yes. The best reason is because any kind of workshop, no matter who runs it or who is in it, is an ideal opportunity for a songwriter to receive priceless feedback on his songs. While it's great if you have friends or family who can give you honest criticism, it's not common. A songwriter's workshop, by its very nature, is a place where people can be honest about other people's songs. Even if you don't agree with the feedback you receive, it will force you to face the way your songs are responded to. It will give you a new perspective on your work that might not be pleasant but will enable you to grow as a writer.

Keep in mind that different people have different songwriting values. For certain songwriters of previous generations, any song lyric that is slightly abstract is to be avoided. Of course, their values were cast in the time of Gershwin and Cole Porter, and they have remained untouched by the expansion of a song's possibilities started in the sixties by Dylan, the Beatles, Simon, and the rest.

At the same time, younger writers have lost sight of many of the great traditional songwriting values and are often impressed by such things as a "great beat" or rhythm track. Be aware of who your audience is but remember that any feedback to your songs, no matter who it comes from, is valid.

Workshops also offer an excellent opportunity to receive professional feedback on your songs. Frequently publishers and producers will run a workshop, and this is a great chance to informally play your material for a professional and receive their feedback. They will analyze your work, no doubt, more on the demands of the marketplace and less on personal musical taste, something friends or family can't offer you.

▼ *How do I find out about songwriter workshops?*

The annual *Songwriter's Market* (published by Writer's Digest Books) has a lengthy chapter listing songwriter associations both in America and England. This is a good place to start. See if there is one near you and if they offer any workshops.

In Los Angeles, The National Academy of Songwriters offers at least two song workshops every week. The Los Angeles Songwriter's Showcase (LASS) offers seminars at their office in L.A. as well as "Pitchathons" in which you can pitch songs directly to publishers. In the fall of every year, LASS offers their Expo, which is a two-day event featuring a huge range of seminars and workshops on every subject important to songwriters. Other workshops in L.A. are held by the Songwriter's Guild of America. ASCAP and BMI hold workshops in Los Angeles, Nashville, and New York. And the Nashville Songwriters Association International offers seminars in Nashville.

It's up to you to contact your regional songwriter associations, many of which offer periodic workshops. Also, local colleges, universities, extension programs, adult education centers, and night schools offer songwriting classes that are essentially workshops. These can be ideal chances to get good feedback on your songs within your community.

▼ *What do I do if there aren't any songwriter groups in my town?*

One alternative to attending workshops is having songs evaluated by the mail. NAS offers what they call the "Out of Area Song Evaluations" for people who live outside of L.A. You mail in your song on cassette with a lyric sheet, and your song will be evaluated by an industry professional. LASS also offers song critiques for members.

Perhaps you should even consider *starting* a songwriting organization in your town. There are many other benefits to belonging to a regional or national songwriter's association besides the workshops. Perhaps the greatest is their ability to remind you that you are not alone in what can often be an extremely lonely pursuit. Knowing that there's a whole community of people nearby who understand your concerns makes this an easier road to go down. It's important to have people in your life who comprehend why you spend your time putting words and music together, and who can discuss the technicalities of it with you. They can offer advice, in both artistic and business matters, and maybe save you a lot of time doing so.

Demos

▼ **I always hear people say that when my song is finished I have to make a good demo. What's a demo?**

"Demo" is short for demonstration, and it refers to making a tape that is essentially a demonstration of a song. A demo is usually a tape made for a publisher, and it is commonly not as elaborate as a finished record of a song. A demo is designed to show off a *song* and not the production.

People make demos for publishers to hear their songs but also for other purposes. Anytime you want someone to hear one of your songs, even if it's simply to critique it, you'll need a demo. An artist who is recording an album might make sketchy, simple demos so that a producer can listen to it and come up with production approaches. Demos are also used to teach songs to back-up musicians.

Some demos are quite straightforward with just piano and voice while others are more elaborate. Today, with the advent of home studios, people are making demos that sound much like finished records.

▼ **I hear a lot of talk about doing "4-track" demos and "8-track" and "24-track." What does this mean and what are the differences between them?**

In the beginning of sound recording, all records were recorded in a mono, or monaural, format.

This means that all sounds are coming from one place, a single source. Stereo, which is short for stereophonic, means that the sound is coming from *two* sources, and that each source has a slightly different combination of sounds so as to create a dimensional effect.

In a stereo setup, you have two separate channels of sound, the left side and the right side. These two sides can also be thought of as tracks, so that a stereo setup is a 2-track format. Any modern stereo tape, album, or CD is in a 2-track format, meaning that two tracks of music are playing at the same time.

Recording studios are equipped with multi-track recording units so that it is possible to record many separate "tracks" of music before combining them all into the normal stereo format for listening. A multi-track setup means that you can record voices on one track, drums on a different track, guitar on a separate track, etc., and then combine those tracks, or "mix" them together into one.

Any format that can record on more than two tracks of music at one time is a multi-track format. After 2-track, there is also a 4-track format, 8-track, 16-track, 24-track and even 48-track. If a studio has a 4-track capability, it means that they can record four separate tracks of music and combine them all into a single whole. An 8-track has eight tracks to use, a 16-track has sixteen, and so on.

Recently there has been a huge increase in the popularity of portable multi-tracks—compact 4-

track cassette machines for the home. With one of these, a songwriter can now have multi-track capabilities in the home without having to buy expensive and sophisticated recording equipment. This allows the songwriter not only to make home demos, but to experiment with songs in the writing process, adding different instruments and harmonies before ever going into a studio.

▼ What is meant by the term "overdubbing"?

To "overdub" means to record something *over* a preexisting track. For example, if you are recording in a 4-track format, you can start by recording a drum machine on one track. After that track is complete, anything that you record onto any of the other tracks is an overdub. If you record a bass to go with the drum pattern, that bass part is an overdub.

The opposite of overdubbing is to record parts simultaneously. The Beatles' landmark *Sgt. Pepper* album was recorded in a 4-track setup. How could this have been possible? How could they have achieved such a sophisticated, multi-layered sound with only four tracks, no more than many songwriters have in their own living rooms? The answer is that many of the initial parts were all recorded simultaneously onto one track. All four Beatles would play at once: Paul on bass, John on rhythm guitar, George on lead, and Ringo on drums (and other combinations). At the same time they might do a lead vocal and some backup harmonies and put all of it on one track. This would leave them three more free tracks for additional overdubbing. And this also explains the magic of the Beatles' records—the music that can be created when musician's interact and play simultaneously is usually more resonant and moving than music made track by track, overdubbing every instrument one at a time.

For a complete look into the Beatles' recording techniques, I highly recommend the book *The Beatles Recording Sessions* by Mark Lewisohn, published by Harmony Books. It's an intensive record of every single recording session the band had from 1962 to 1970, detailing who played what on the basic tracks as well as on the overdubs. It's an inspiring, historical work which proves that it is pos-

sible to capture magic on tape and to do wonderful songs justice.

▼ How good does a demo have to be to submit it to a publisher? Is it okay to do a piano/voice demo?

Unfortunately, a piano/voice or guitar/voice demo will not be sufficiently impressive for most music publishers these days unless you already have some kind of track record. Time was when a publisher could hear a song in its barest form and see potential in it. Nowadays, however, many publishers have little if any musical imagination since their expertise is in business, not music. The publisher must be able to hear a song as a potential radio song, a song that could get radio play. And that is essentially all they care about.

While a demo for a publisher needn't be a finished, fully produced single, it should have the trappings of a record—a drum beat (either by live drums or a drum machine), a bass line (by a bass, either acoustic or electric, or a synth), guitar and/or keyboards, a good, clear vocal, and maybe some harmonies.

As publishers are especially concerned with the chorus, or "hook" of the song, it's important that you make this section crystal clear in your production. You want to make it possible for a publisher to hear your song and recognize the chorus the first time they hear it without looking at the lyric sheet.

To accomplish this, you need to punch up your chorus. The easiest way to do this is to make the rest of the production fairly sparse up to that point. Don't use all tracks or all instruments at once; it's more effective for a song to build in intensity. This buildup should be written into the song: verses should build and lead into the chorus. But you can also build the intensity with the production.

▼ ────────────────────

Listen to any record by Steely Dan. Although they utilize a big barrage of colors with keyboards, horns, guitars, drums, bass, vocals, and more, the sound is never heavy because all of the parts interweave. Instead of having everything happen at once, the instruments are used sparingly and there is space between the parts; a sax might appear when needed and then disappear again for many measures, just as guitar lines will be woven in only when needed. It's easy to have all the instruments play on every measure but far more effective when the parts are balanced.

Listen also to reggae music for a great example of how to space instrumental parts. Notice the way the separate parts, such as the bass and guitars, are present but not overbearing. They have a specific role to play and do not move beyond that role.

Like painting, if you mix all colors together at the same time, the result will be mud. To keep your music from being muddy, be aware of which sounds cancel the others and which ones blend.

For example, begin the song only with a vocal, drums, bass, and one chordal instrument—piano, keyboard, or guitar. Then, when the chorus arrives, add more layers for emphasis. Synth pads—a string sound or horn patch, for example—are ideal for this purpose as they add color and power to a section. Harmonies are also ideal, especially if we haven't heard them before in the song. And the addition of any other instrument in the chorus will serve the same purpose, to punch up the chorus so that there is no mistaking when it arrives.

At the same time, it's important to remember that production cannot make a weak song strong. It's the words and the music that are the most important aspects, and if there is any weakness there, production will not help. You do not want to mask or hide qualities that are in your song, you want to enhance them. Ideally, production can take whatever strengths are built into a song via the writing, and amplify them.

▼

Steve Schalchlin, the writer of *SongTalk*'s "Forum" column, offers this advice: "Don't be afraid to go back to your original rough recording of a song for reference if you find yourself 'lost' in some overblown arrangement. Strip it down to the bone and start over if it doesn't *feel* right.

"If you are paying a studio to make your demo, *never assume the person behind the board*

knows more about your song than you do."

It's easy for a songwriter to fall into the trap of going into a recording studio and being intimidated into producing a song in a way that is simply wrong for the tune. I once brought in a simple ballad to a producer at a studio, knowing the song needed little more than piano, bass, drums, and a good vocal to be effective. The producer felt compelled to add an entire section onto the end of the song replete with near-screaming female backup vocals. It was entirely inappropriate for the song, and when I listen to it now I'm amazed that I ever agreed to let it be produced in that way. At the time, though, he convinced me that by adding this section we would liven up the song without taking away any of its strengths. He was wrong. Having that weird, extra section at the end of the song destroyed the balance of the song's sections, and changed the entire emphasis and focus of the words.

The point is that a songwriter must trust his or her own instincts about a song. It's your kid, after all, you raised him yourself. Are you going to let some stranger dress him? How can somebody else possibly know what would be right for your own flesh and blood? A song is every bit as much your creation as is a child (and maybe even more, as songs don't require two people to create them). Understand that as the sole creator of a piece of work, you are in the best position to judge what is right for that work. While it makes sense to listen to as much advice as possible from others about how to produce a song, make sure that the final decision is entirely yours, and that it's a decision that enables the song itself—and not the production—to shine.

Jeff "Skunk" Baxter, formerly of Steely Dan and the Doobie Brothers, said this at an NAS *SongTalk* seminar: "As songwriters, we are all little companies putting out a product and we are trying to get big companies interested in buying our product. That means that we must be smart salesmen and make it easy and possible for the buyer to hear and appreciate our product. But all the pretty packaging in the world won't sell a bad product."

▼ *Is a good vocal important for demo tapes?*

Of course. When making demo tapes for publishers, it makes sense to mix the vocal even higher than you would normally if you were making a record so that the lyrics are easily discernible. If you aren't a great singer yourself—or if your voice is not the ideal one to sell the song—find a singer who can do the song justice. There are countless vocalists who will sing on demos in exchange for a copy of the tape that they can then use as their own demo for their own purposes.

▼ *I have a 4-track cassette setup at home. Is that a good enough system to record a song demo on?*

Yes. Of course, it depends on how well you can record with your system. Having a decent drum machine and some good microphones will make a huge difference in terms of sound quality as well as some kind of a delay system to add echo or delay to the vocals.

You'll also need a decent 2-track machine (a regular cassette recorder) to mix your 4-track down. You can make an excellent 4-track demo, but unless you mix it down on a decent machine, the result will be full of hiss or distortion. Listen closely to your mixed-down tape to ensure that it's clear and understandable.

▼ *But why do I have to mix down from my 4-track if it's already on cassette? Can't I send this cassette to someone just as it is?*

No. A 4-track cassette machine works by playing both sides of a cassette at once. Every cassette has two tracks on each side; these two tracks are used for stereo, for the left and right channels. A 4-track will play all four tracks at the same time.

A regular cassette player only plays two tracks at any one time. If you were to take a tape you recorded in a 4-track machine and put it in a normal machine (like if you played it in your car stereo), you will only hear two of the four tracks.

The solution is simple: you simultaneously record all four tracks at once onto *another* cassette tape, a standard 2-track. This process is known as a mixdown—"mixing" refers to the adjustment of

levels on all your tracks. While mixing down, you can experiment with the various levels on every track so that the mix of the tracks is effective: you want the vocal to be heard above all, but you also want a nice mixture of bass and drums and your other instruments.

Some of this mixing might already be done if you have bounced any tracks prior to this point.

▼ *What is meant by "bouncing" tracks?*

"Bouncing" refers to combining tracks on one recording machine before you do a mixdown. For example, if you have a 4-track setup, you can record more than four tracks by the use of bouncing. Here's how: First you record three tracks. Say you record a drum machine on track one, a bass on track two, and a guitar on track three. You can then combine these tree tracks and "bounce" all of them together to track four, which is the only remaining open track. You would then have drum machine, bass, and guitar all combined on track four, and you can record other things on tracks one, two, and three. (The technical methods for bouncing differ for each system though the concept is the same; check your manual for instructions.)

While bouncing, keep in mind that the overall sound quality is diminished each time you bounce. The bass end of the spectrum, especially, can get easily lost in a bounce. To compensate you can record the initial bass track a little hotter than you ordinarily would.

When doing a bounce you have to be as conscious of adjusting all the levels (bass, treble, and volume) as carefully as when you are mixing. And like mixing, you want to make sure that your bounce is acceptable so you have to listen to it carefully before you record anything over your original tracks. If a bounce doesn't work well—if the drums are too loud, for example—you rebounce it as many times as you need to until you get it right. Of course, once you record over an original track, you can no longer go back and rebounce. So make sure you get your bounce sounding perfect before you move on.

You can do more than one bounce. For example, if you bounce three tracks to track four (as in our previous example), you can record new instruments on tracks one and two and then bounce those, with track four, onto track three. In this way, you can bounce indefinitely, but each time you do so the sound quality is greatly diminished. Attempting to do more than two bounces on a 4-track is not advisable if you want a clear, usable demo. If you're just doing it to experiment or for your own amusement, go for it! And have fun.

You can also do bounces on 8-track machines or any other multi-track system. When you start working on 16-track systems or more, however, your need to bounce is obviously lessened.

It's also possible on a multi-track system to do what is called a "sub-mix." This differs from a bounce in that you mix some but not all of the tracks to a single track. For example, in a 16-track studio you might want to record the drums on ten tracks at once to get a full sound. You record the bass drum on one track, the snare on one track, the high-hat on one track, etc., so that you can then have full control over the mix of the whole drum kit. You can then do a "sub-mix" of these tracks, recording them all down to two tracks so that you can have the sound of well-recorded drums in stereo as well as fourteen more open tracks.

▼ What do I need to make my 4-track recordings at home sound professional?

In addition to your 4-track machine, you need some instruments first of all. A guitar or piano can be used as the basic chordal instrument, while bass can be provided either on an actual bass—electric or acoustic—or on a synthesizer. For drums you need a drum machine unless you have the space for live drums as well as the access to a drummer. If you are not a proficient singer, or if your voice is not right for a particular song, you need to find the right singer or singers for your project.

You need at least one decent microphone and preferably more. These are for recording vocals and also for recording any instruments that you don't record directly. For example, an electric guitar can plug in directly to your 4-track or you can plug it into an amp and mike the amp. An acoustic guitar, and other acoustic instruments such as drums or piano, need to be miked.

You need some kind of delay or echo system for vocals, primarily, and also for use on other tracks. (A decent digital delay unit that has different settings for delay functions can be purchased for about two hundred dollars and up.)

If you are going to use a drum machine instead of a drummer, you need a decent-sounding one: some of them can sound very cheesy and cheap. Running the drum machine through a decent delay will also add a world of difference.

If you are planning to record live drums, you need the space to do so, and this means sound-proofing the room if your studio is anywhere near civilization. And to mike live drums well, you need at least three well-placed microphones.

You need a good cassette machine, apart from your 4-track machine for mixing-down from your 4-track tape, as previously described. No matter how well you record your 4-track master, the quality of the demo is still dependent on this machine. If it is not a great one, or if, for example, its tape heads are unclean, it will add a tremendous amount of hiss and distortion to the sound of your demo.

A synthesizer of some sort can add a great amount to a home demo. While it is rare to have a string section, a horn section, or a Hammond organ in the home, a decent synth can provide a workable substitute for all of them. It can also give you a good bass (especially nice if you don't play bass but also good simply for a different bass effect), percussion sounds, and an unlimited amount of sounds that you can create on your own to add textures to your recording.

A synth combined with acoustic instruments can sound especially nice; mixing it in with acoustic piano and guitar on a track can add a new dimension to a song.

▼ What kind of tapes should I use? And how do I get tape copies made?

Always use high-quality, high-bias tapes both for your masters and for your copies. Ideally, your tape will get played many times and each time it gets played, the magnetic information on it gets a little jumbled. Protect your song from disintegration by investing in the best tapes you can. Also, steer clear of super short tapes even if you only need the tape for a single song. Longer tapes—60-

minute tapes or 90-minute tapes—always have better quality, while the short ones can wear out quickly. Shorter tapes are great when submitting a song for a competition, or for some other purpose in which it won't get played many times.

For tape copies, look in local entertainment magazines or the Yellow Pages for audio tape duplication. There are many places in most cities that do cassette duplications from both reel-to-reel master tapes and from cassettes. Most of these places offer both real-time and fast-speed duplication. Fast speed is a less expensive process in which tapes are duplicated at a faster than normal speed. While it obviously takes less time to use this process and enables you to make more copies in a shorter period of time, the quality is not as good as with real-time copies. Make real-time copies for your most important tapes: If they are for publishers, producers, record companies, etc., you want it to sound as clear as possible. Only duplicate the tapes yourself if you have quality recording equipment at home.

▼ I want to produce my own demo, but I don't have any home demo capabilities. What should I do?

You should check into recording studios in your area. For a demo, an 8-track studio is quite sufficient. There's no need to go to a larger, more expensive studio, such as 16-track or 24-track, if you are recording demos. Those studios exist primarily for the recording of actual masters for record albums.

▼ What should I look for in a recording studio?

To find a studio that is right for your work, you should check many things. You want to make sure that you hear an example of a tape that has been recorded there. It's important that they can produce a clear, clean, high-fidelity demo.

Talk to the engineer at the studio who would handle your project. Is he/she someone with whom you can easily communicate? What kind of music do they usually record at the studio? For example, if you are planning to record a ballad, does this engineer have any experience recording softer mu-

sic or has he primarily worked with heavy metal bands?

Check out the facility in general. Is the control room in good shape or is there a snarl of wires and electronics all over the place? Does the studio have ample space for your needs? If you are planning to record live drums, do they have any experience doing so? Keep in mind that so much recording has been done in the past years using drum machines that many engineers haven't the slightest idea how to record live drums, let alone the space necessary to do so. On the other hand, some studios have ample space and even a drum booth perfect for recording drums.

Do they have good microphones? Any decent studio should be able to offer somewhat of a variety of microphones to use both for vocals and for miking live instruments. A Schure microphone is the most common one, but it's a good sign if a studio owns any microphones by Sennheiser, Neumann, or AKG.

Do they have a decent acoustic piano? If they say, "No, but don't worry—I can get a great piano sound on my synth," decide if you need acoustic piano or not. If you do need it, find a studio with a real piano; don't settle for less than what you need.

Do they have any other musical instruments? Most studios these days—even small 8-track "demo" studios—have a few synthesizers, maybe a piano, maybe an electric guitar, and more. If they have a MIDI-synth set up, for example, you will be able to create a much fuller, richer sound with a few tracks than you would be able to do without MIDI capabilities.

Is the environment of the studio itself conducive to good work for you? Since this is a place where you will probably spend many long hours working, it has to be a place where you can feel comfortable enough to do good work.

Do they have some good outboard gear? This refers to the equipment they have for affecting recorded sounds: delay systems, compressors, echo plates, etc. A small studio with good outboard gear can make tapes that sound every bit as professional as those made at larger studios if (and this is a big "if") the engineer knows how best to use them.

Joe Borja, an independent recording engineer

in L.A. who has recorded numerous albums, advises the beginning songwriter to be aware of the following things when approaching a recording studio for the first time: "If you walk into the control room, you can be dazzled by lights and gizmos, it's like Star Trek. But in fact, one out of three might not work, they're just lit. Many of the cheaper studios have more glitz than substance, so don't be fooled by lots of lights.

"A studio should have at least four good limiters and compressors. They should have a least one tube mike for vocals and at least a full complement of dynamic mikes for guitars and drums—if they have more than what you need, you're in good shape. If they only have four mikes you're in trouble, and a lot of expensive studios have only four mikes.

"Another good thing to check is if the control room is clean. If it's not, you know that the maintenance is not first-rate. This is a place where you need to be creative and make your own mess. If there's a mess to begin with, that's not good.

"Make sure that the engineer has experience and is someone that you can work with. No matter how good the studio is, if you can't communicate your ideas to the engineer, and if he can't carry them out, your project will not be successful."

▼ *Once I find a good recording studio where I feel I can work, how should I prepare for the date?*

"The key is preproduction," Borja answers. "By that I mean planning out everything you are going to do beforehand so that you don't waste precious studio time. No one can stress that enough. Get you ideas sorted out before you go in there. Find someone who can help you out if this is your first time. Your first recording experience may result in more of an experience for you than a recording. But you can learn from your mistakes and there's no way to learn except by doing.

"A basic plan of attack is to have a schedule to start with to give you an idea of how you want to spend your day. Experimenting is a luxury that's not really affordable the first time around, because before you know it, your time is used up.

"Go to a friend's house who has a 4-track and do your experimenting at that stage. Harmonies are the hardest thing to do your first time in a studio. You can spend six hours on background harmonies to a lead vocal that may or may not work, so work out your harmonies in advance."

▼ *How long should a one-song demo take?*

If you are not going to use live drums, the entire process will not take as long and you can save money. Is the sound of live drums necessary for your particular song? It's up to you to decide, based both on your aesthetic and economic sensibilities. Many studios nowadays have MIDI/computer setups that are ideal for producing fast and inexpensive songwriter demos. With these systems, all the parts are preprogrammed so that the actual recording time is minimal. You have to determine if this kind of production is suitable both for your song and your budget.

The scenario described by Joe Borja in the following applies to recording demos in a studio with live drums and other live instruments as opposed to preprogramming the parts.

"The basic setup time takes an hour for setting up mikes and getting the drum machine aligned. Figure half an hour to get the drums sounding right. Go with simplicity, make the drum kit as simple as possible. For a song demo, the drum tracks should be as simple as possible. If you are using a drum machine, which is okay for song demos, you don't need as much setup time. After that, the basic track shouldn't take more than an hour and a half. By that, I mean drums, bass, and guitar or keyboard.

"Vocals should take about three hours if they all are rehearsed before you go into a studio. The remaining time is about two hours for more guitars or keys to augment the song; three hours to mix, depending on the engineer. A good engineer can do it in a half hour."

Adding this up: one hour set up, a half hour for drum setup, an hour and a half for basic tracks, three hours for vocals, about an hour for augmenting the tracks, and three hours for mixdown, you've got a total of ten hours to demo one song. It seems like a lot of time, and it is. Keep in mind that Borja, a perfectionist, has very high standards and so is figuring in extra time to make sure he gets everything just right. For a simple song demo, especially without the use of live drums, you can record in far less time.

Many studios will offer a per-song rate, and this is often the best route to go. If you pay per song instead of by the hour, you will not have to watch the clock and be pressured by the passage of time.

Studio rates

This brings us to Borja's next point: find a studio with good rates.

"Talk to a studio about its block rates," Borja says, meaning the kind of deal you can get for a ten-hour block of time rather than an hourly rate. "Also, talk to them about their downtime. This is the time when the studio is booked for someone who can't come in, and you can often get downtime at a much reduced rate."

And what does Borja feel are reasonable studio rates? "For 8-track, not more than fifteen dollars an hour. For 16-track not more than twenty dollars an hour, and for 24-track a rate of twenty-five dollars an hour is fair. Think in terms of ten- and twelve-hour blocks. It's hard to get much done in smaller periods of time.

"Smaller studios should be willing to help you out in terms of rates," Borja continues. "The rates should fit your budget."

▼ What else do I need to know when making demos?

"The most important thing is to hook up with someone who has some engineering experience. Find someone who has some expertise in the studio and listen to that person."

While Borja uses live drums on almost all of his recording dates, he emphasized that for song demos the use of drum machines is perfectly acceptable. However, if you are going to use a live drummer, he suggested using a click track. (A click track is simply a track that contains a steady count that sets the tempo; essentially it is the sound of a mechanical metronome ticking out the beats of each measure.) "Using a click track is really important," Borja says. "It's really good to have some sort of time base there so you can gauge how the tune is progressing. The song can do a roller coaster

without a click track, and you won't be aware of it until you try to do the other tracks."

Attempting to produce a clean demo using live drums, I once brought in a friend who I thought was a talented drummer. And he was talented, though deficient in the tempo department, meaning that his time would fluctuate. Trying to overdub other parts on top of that fluctuating drum track was not only difficult, but impossible to perfect. After trying many hours to get it right, we settled on a track that was not "in the pocket" and ultimately ineffective.

Another suggestion that Joe Borja gave was to work out the vocals in advance so as not to have to sing them too many times in the studio. "People run into a cardboard situation," he said. "By that I mean, if you say 'cardboard, cardboard, cardboard' after a while it becomes a sound—two syllables—and not a word. It's easy to get caught up with trying to perfect a vocal track, while it's more important to get the lyrics across and keep the passion intact."

▼ What makes a professional-sounding demo?

A professional-sounding demo is well recorded, has a strong and prominent vocal (or vocals), and a musical foundation that is solid and not overdone.

You can make a professional-sounding demo either at a studio or on home equipment. Either way you go, your goal should be to get a clear-sounding, undistorted recording of your song that is low in tape hiss, and has strong low-, middle-, and upper-range dynamics.

Vocals

The vocal on a demo must be prominent, even more so than on an album. This is because you are selling the song in a demo, not the artist, and the words must be clear, up front, and on tune. So make sure that your singer, whether it's you or someone else, is a strong vocalist, able to enunciate clearly and to emotionally connect with the heart of the song. The latter part is key, as even a trained vocalist will not do justice to a song without some emotional connection. (A good idea is to discuss the lyrics and thrust of a song with a singer so they know the right attitude to adopt.)

Mixing

Make sure when you are mixing your demo that the vocal is easy to hear. If it is too far back into the musical track the words will be lost. The voice will also be obscured by other frequencies that get in the way. Cymbal crashes, extensive use of high-hat, and an overbearing snare crash (a frequent offender) can all take up frequencies that should be left open for the voice. You want to cushion and support the vocal with the musical track, not drown it.

The bottom end

To get a solid musical foundation to support the vocal, you need a bottom end, a middle range, and an upper end. The bottom end is provided by the drums and bass. The bass supports the lower end of the harmonic structure of the song while the drums sustain the rhythm of the song. It's advisable to make sure that the drums and bass are perfectly in place before attempting to add the other pieces. To get a track that is especially tight with a clean bottom end, the bass part should work with the bass drum pattern, either matching it rhythmically or weaving it into the bass line. Otherwise the result will be muddy and indistinct. If the bass-line is going to be more melodic and less restricted to a supporting role, use the upper range of the instrument when possible so as not to clash with the drums.

Trying to overdub drums onto an existing track recorded without a strict rhythm will always spell trouble. Say you have recorded guitar and voice and you want to add the drums. Unless your tempo was perfect in playing that guitar and singing the vocal—as unwavering as a metronome—it will be quite difficult for a drummer to supply an even rhythm, and the result will be a foundation that isn't solid.

Trying to overdub a drum machine onto an existing instrumental track that is not perfectly in time is simply impossible because a drum machine can only play patterns in perfect time. (The exception is if you play the machine manually live onto a track as opposed to programming it with patterns

as is usually done.) It has no ability technologically thus far in time to adapt to a human tempo, though progress is being made in this direction. Most machines play time as perfectly as a metronome. All the more reason to record the drum track first, as it will keep the rest of the instruments in tempo.

The middle range

The middle range of the recording can be provided by a rhythm instrument playing the chord changes of a song, be it guitar, piano, synth, or some combination of these. Horn and string sections can also provide middle range, but in a demo it's more economical and easier to use a synthesizer for this purpose.

The middle-range instruments can be recorded at the same time as you record the bass and drums, so as to guide them. Often people will play a "scratch" guitar or drum track along with the bass and drums to get them in place and then replace it later with a perfect guitar or piano part.

The high end

The high end of the recording is provided most prominently by the vocals. Other touches can also be added to the high end, making sure it doesn't get cluttered—the vocal must not have to compete. But woven around a vocal line, and in sections in which there are no vocals, you can fill in the high end with the use of lead guitar (both electric and acoustic), use of horns (sax is especially adaptable to songs, while other wind instruments, like clarinet, trumpet, and flute, can add their own unique presence to a song), harmony and supporting vocals, percussion and other instrumental touches I will leave up to your imagination to suggest. For example, a touch of bagpipes on one section or the subtle use of a spectral musical saw can add a whole new dimension to the song. Remember, though, that you are making a demo to sell a song, not a band or instrumentalist. If you know a killer sax player, don't include a four-minute sax solo in the middle of the song to show him off. Let him do that on his tape. Use his talent to enhance your song without detracting from it.

As mentioned previously, another thing to watch out for in terms of not cluttering up the high end of a recording is the drummer's use of cymbals. If you are using a drum machine, you control the use of cymbals yourself. But a live drummer often relies heavily on his cymbals to fill out his drum sound, and these cymbals can get in the way of all the high frequencies on the tape. You have to make sure your drummer uses them sparingly in the right places.

One solution to this problem was offered by Peter Gabriel, who actually removed the cymbals from the studio, reasoning that if they are there, the drummer is going to use them. You might not want to be that extreme (at the risk of angering your drummer), but do be careful.

The finished demo

When all of these pieces are in place—the high, middle, and lower ranges of your recording—and your vocals are clear and out front, pay attention to the overall combined sounds of these parts. Is there any distortion of sound when there is a volume increase? Is there an abundant amount of audible tape hiss? Are all of the parts easy to hear? Are the bass and drums present and clean without being overbearing? Is there an overall feeling of cohesion? When you have asked all of these questions and analyzed the answers to your satisfaction, you have a finished demo.

▼ **Not only don't I have a home studio, I don't have the expertise to go to an outside recording studio to produce a demo. What should I do?**

There are many excellent demo services around the country that you can use for a reasonable price. These are places that will do all the work for you: all you have to do is send or bring in your song (on tape or on sheet music; if on tape, the simplest version will be sufficient, even a voice with no other instrumental backing), and they will produce and record your demo for you.

Naturally, some of these services are better than others, so be sure that you check them out as thoroughly as possible before beginning to do business with them. As with a studio, start by requesting examples of their work to see for yourself

the kind of treatment they give songs and if it would be suitable for your own work.

The three most important things to consider when checking out a demo service are price, time, and quality.

As far as price goes, I've found that one hundred dollars for a single song is fair (as of this writing) if the production is sufficient. By this I mean a good vocal, drums, bass, and guitar or piano. A piano/voice or guitar/voice vocal is not sufficient.

As far as time, find out how long it will take for you to get a finished product back after sending in your tape. Some places will claim to take two months—a long enough time to wait—and then can take twice that long before sending you the finished demo. Get in writing an estimated time of completion so that you won't be left hanging. It's also advisable to call references to find out how long it took them to get their demos finished. A wait any longer than two months is quite unnecessary; if that demo service is too busy to get it back to you any sooner, find another one. Some services can actually turn over tapes in one week's time. Make sure you get an agreement in terms of time up front before beginning the project.

As far as quality, you want to make sure that your songs can be produced in a clear, professional-sounding way. There's no way to know for sure if your song will get a proper treatment except by trying it once. You should always make sure that you hear examples of previous demos that the company has produced. You also want to make sure that you find a demo service that is suitable to your specific style. For example, if you write country songs, there are many good demo services in Nashville that might be perfect for your music. If you are writing songs in a rock vein, ask to hear examples of demos created in that genre. Make sure, especially, that the chosen vocalist has a voice and style suitable to your song. A rock song sung in a Vegas-like, lounge-lizard style will not work.

For demo service referrals or to check if a demo service is legitimate, you can call the National Academy of Songwriters at (800) 826-7287 outside of California and (800) 334-1446 in California. You can also call the Studio Referral Service in Los Angeles at (818) 508-8828.

Publishing

▼ What is a music publisher?

A music publisher is a person in the business of finding songs, and attempting to get those songs recorded by artists.

The songwriter is the creator of a song. He has every right to serve as his own publisher; there is no obligation to have a song published by an outside publisher and it requires no license to become a publisher.

The publisher owns and controls the copyright of the song. If your song is published by a publisher other than yourself, you as the songwriter relinquish your control over the use of a copyright. This means that the publisher will make the decisions as to who the song is pitched to and how it can be used.

▼ What purpose does a music publisher serve for a songwriter?

Unlike a publisher of literature who can publish a book or magazine himself and distribute that product, a music publisher has the job of not only finding a suitable product but also of placing that product: finding some use for it that will generate income. Therefore, the music publisher's main service for the songwriter is in the *placing* of her song (on a record, in a movie, etc.). Once a song is recorded and distributed, then there is a market for the sheet music, although this market is nowhere as large as it used to be back in the days of crowd-ing around the old piano and singing the standards of the day.

Publishers also serve as administrators for a songwriter. Besides placing the song, they can do the paperwork, the administration involved with the collection of royalties for the song, as well as serving as the representative for the songwriter for any potential uses of the song.

▼ What kind of a demo package should I put together for a publisher?

It's advisable to put together the most professional package you can, keeping in mind how other demo packages will compete with yours for a publisher's attention. It doesn't take that much to appear professional.

1. Never include more than three songs on a cassette tape.

2. Make sure that the names of the song are clearly written or typed on the front of the tape itself.

3. Make sure that your copyright symbol with your name and the current year appears on the front of the tape. (If a song was actually written seven years ago, there's no need to write that year on the tape. Always use the current year. You don't want to give the impression to a publisher that you are giving him an old song that has been sitting

around for years and that nobody has had any interest in. You want to give the impression of coming in with new, fresh material.) On the back of the tape, write your name (and your collaborators' names if there are any), and your telephone number. If the tape is separated from the lyric sheet—which is likely—a publisher will be able to easily track it to you.

4. Enclose a single, typed lyric sheet for each song. Lyrics should be double-spaced, and choruses should always be indented. Publishers don't always (if ever) listen all the way to the end of most songs. But if the chorus is indented and clearly marked, you'll have a better chance of having the song heard at least through to the chorus. And if they like the chorus they might listen further.

5. Use capital letters and lower-case letters when typing your lyrics. Some writers feel that it looks more impressive to use all capitals, but actually IT LOOKS KIND OF DUMB WHEN EVERY SINGLE WORD OF A SONG IS WRITTEN IN CAPITAL LETTERS. IT SEEMS AS IF SOMEONE IS SHOUTING. Stick to normal type.

6. Write a *very* short cover letter, introducing yourself as the writer, listing the songs and giving some casting ideas (see the sample). Don't take up the publisher's time by writing long stories about the song, why they are important, the inspiration behind them, etc. Your song has got to speak for itself. If the song doesn't work based solely on how it sounds and how it is written, no amount of letter-writing will help. If it needs a preamble or an explanation of any kind to be effective, that is a sure sign that there is a weakness in the song and it is in need of a rewrite.

7. If you have stationery with a letterhead, use it. Again, you want to appear as professional as possible, and a letterhead with your name or the name of your "company" (if your name is Smith, you can call your company Smithsongs, for example) will make it appear that songwriting for you is a business, not a hobby. Publishers want to work with professionals, not hobbyists.

8. Enclose a self-addressed, stamped envelope big enough and with sufficient postage for a publisher to mail back your tape. Don't expect to get it back if you don't carry out this step.

9. It's not necessary to use a tape case, and they can make mailing bulky. Most publishers prefer if you wrap the lyric sheet around the tape, and secure it with a rubber band.

And that's all! Again, don't give the publishers any more than they need—the tape, the lyric sheet, and the shortest possible cover letter will do it. Some songwriters believe that even a cover letter is too much, that the tape and the song should speak for itself. I don't agree, as a tape package is going to be impersonal enough; a short letter reminds the publisher of the person involved. But understand the concern—you don't want the publisher to be bogged down with papers. You want him to get to that song and its lyric sheet as easily as possible. Don't put anything else in his way, and keep that cover letter as to-the-point as possible. Here's an example that you can use with your own specifics, of course.

Dear Mr. Pincus,

My name is George Burakowski and I'm a songwriter living in Tucson, Arizona. Enclosed please find a tape and lyric sheet for my song "Swimming with Horses" for your consideration. I think it would be ideal for either Willie Nelson or Randy Travis.

Thank you and I look forward to hearing from you.

Sincerely,

George Burakowski

▼ If I only put three songs on my demo, should I save my best song for last?

No. Put your best song first. Publishers often don't listen to entire tapes. If they aren't entranced, interested, or hooked in somewhat by that very first song they hear, chances are that your tape might be quickly discarded. You have to figure out not only which song is best but which is most commercial and accessible. Once you get a publisher on your side, then you can risk being more challenging. But you have to do what you can to get his attention in the first place.

▼ Is mailing in a demo the best way to go about it? Wouldn't it be better to go into a publisher's office in person?

It depends on the nature of the publisher. Some would prefer if you sent a tape first as a means of introduction, and this is probably a good idea. But by all means, a personal appointment with a publisher in which you can meet face-to-face can be much more effective than sending a tape in the mail. It's also a good deal scarier as it will usually lead to quicker rejections and the overall humiliation of sitting across from a publisher, having him put your heart's work into a tape machine, listen to a minute of it, and say something along the lines of, "I don't hear it," or "It's nice but it's not what I need right now. Bring me a hit." This kind of experience can break a songwriter's spirit. If you want to succeed in this field, you have to be able to sit through that kind of treatment and be ready to start again tomorrow. Because tomorrow might be the day when a publisher says, "Yeah! I want this one."

▼ How do you make appointments to meet with music publishers?

Check out which publishers are in the city where you live. New York, L.A., and Nashville are the primary music centers in America, but other major cities also have their share of publishers.

Call the publisher's office, ask if they are accepting outside material for review, and if so, ask to make a personal appointment. Many times the secretary might tell you to send in a tape by mail. But there are a good number of publishers still willing to meet personally with writers. After all, it is their business to meet and encourage new writers. You are potentially a major money-maker for a publisher.

If you are able to make a personal appointment, bring in your three best songs. Record each one of them onto a separate tape, so as to save the time of cuing up songs and searching tapes. Remember that his time—like yours—is money, so waste none of it. If he doesn't like the first song he hears, rather than making him search through a tape, give him the next tape with the next song cued up and ready to go and accompanied by a lyric sheet. (Sheet music is almost never necessary as few publishers nowadays can read music.)

▼ ─────────────────────────

It's advisable when bringing in a song personally to a publisher to have a few casting ideas for the song, some idea of an artist or artists to whom the song can be pitched. Just as you don't want to depend on a publisher's imagination by providing him with an underproduced demo, you want to provide him with casting ideas to make his job easier. If you have artists in mind who the song is suitable for, you can say, "I think this would be ideal for Kenny Rogers, though I could also hear Amy Grant and Kim Carnes singing it," it will be easier for the publisher to conceive of the song getting recorded. If, however, he gives you a blank expression and says, "It's nice, but who can you hear doing it?" and you have no names on the tip of your tongue, you'll show him how hard a job it would be to get the song covered, since even its writer can't think of anyone who could sing it. Do your homework and be ready with answers.

───────────────────────── ▲

Another good idea is to get to know the person at the front desk of whatever company you are approaching. Not only might that person have more influence than you might ever imagine, they can also serve as a great fount of specific knowledge. For example, if you get to know the person fairly well, you can ask them such questions as "What kinds of songs does he really like? What kinds of songs does he hate? What's the best thing to do to impress him? What would make the best impression on him?" As Steve Schalchlin of NAS said, "Look at that person as an open door, not as an armed guard trying to keep you out."

Remember, though, that none of this will help if your songs are not good. There's no need spending much energy marketing your songs if they are not ready for the market and need further development. At the same time, many songwriters write brilliant songs and never market them, preferring to stay in the comfortable world of the artist and away from the world of commerce. It's an understandable desire: if we had wanted to be businessmen, we would have gone into business and not music. But to make a living as a songwriter, or even to get on the road leading to that place, it takes blowing your own horn and pushing your songs into the world. It's not fun, certainly not as much fun as writing, but it's necessary. So many great songs remain unheard while mediocre ones are played around the world because the writers of the lesser songs were great at marketing themselves, making the connections, and having the chutzpah.

Experience teaches us that even the greatest songwriters could count on nobody besides themselves to sell their songs. From Burt Bacharach through Sammy Fain to Jimmy Webb and beyond, even those writers with an outstanding, proven track record still have to push their own songs. And like a salesman, you've got to sell that publisher on not only the song, but on you as the writer.

Lamont Dozier believes "Writers should spend as much time marketing their songs as writing, if not more. You have to keep the deal you've made with yourself to get the song out. No stone should go unturned.

"You have to know everything you can about the workings of the business. You have to do it all yourself. There's so much competition, so many people wanting to get into this business, that you have to make sure you are on top of your affairs. You can't leave it to anyone else."

▼ *What's the best time to meet with music publishers?*

If you are going to make an appointment, always avoid Mondays, as they follow weekends and might find people in a less than energetic mood. Along the same line, avoid Friday afternoons as people might be distracted by upcoming weekend plans. It's best to aim for midweek, late morning or early afternoon, when people are the most awake and alert. And make sure you are punctual. Never keep a publisher waiting; the last thing you want to do is be responsible in any way for the publisher to be in a bad mood.

If you are in a city that has any functions for songwriters, such as seminars or workshops, it's a great idea to take advantage of those kind of situations to meet music publishers on neutral ground. If you can actually get to know a publisher on a personal basis—so that they think of you as a person and not simply as another hungry songwriter—you'll have an easier time when it comes to bringing in a song. Take advantage of every networking type situation that comes your way, and get to know as many publishers and people in the industry as possible.

▼ _____

"Schmoozing" is a word that implies superficial mingling. The hope is that a writer's work will speak for itself and no amount of schmoozing will help. But, in fact, getting to know people in the business, and getting people on your side, is necessary. No songwriter can make it on his own without some support in the industry. Schmoozing alone will not get you anywhere as a writer: If you get some industry attention and then your work is unworthy, you've wasted your time. It's the old story of always being ready; if that schmoozing leads to some solid connections, you had better be ready with solidly produced tapes of solidly written songs or your efforts will be in vain.

A Yiddish word that comes into play here is "chutzpah." It basically means having a lot of nerve. It takes a lot of chutzpah to arrange an appointment with a publisher, just as it is needed at a seminar, workshop, or conference to go up to a publisher and introduce yourself as a talented songwriter. But this is what it takes. It's not easy—it's much easier to be persistent and pushy on someone else's behalf, or on behalf of some cause. But when it comes to pushing one's own career or one's own songs, you are in the position of saying, "This is Me. These are My songs written by Me. And I'm great. I want you to put your faith in Me." You have to blow your own horn, and it's not an easy thing to do. But this is the path you've chosen as a songwriter and this is what is required. So if you're shy—and most artists and performers are shy—work on increasing your own personal level of chutzpah.

_____ ▲

▼ *What are publishers looking for in songs?*

When you ask publishers this question, they often give the same answer: "I'm looking for hits. Bring me a hit." Of course, they never answer the obvious follow-up question, "What makes a hit?" And the reason they don't answer that question is because nobody really knows the answer. So many unusual, against-the-rules songs have become major hits that there is no easy formula by which to determine what a hit is or can be. In 1989 two very unusual songs competed at the Grammys for best song. One was "Fast Car" by Tracy Chapman, an acoustically based folksong dealing with some tough realities of urban life. It was certainly not a song that most publishers would consider to be commercial. The other song, the one that won the Grammy, was "Don't Worry, Be Happy" by Bobby McFerrin, which is essentially a simple ditty recorded completely a capella, using only McFerrin's amazing voice instead of any instruments. It's the kind of song that if you brought it into a publisher, he would say, "Yeah, it's nice, but I don't know what to do with it."

Which brings us to the crux of this problem. Publishers don't know what will be a hit tomorrow but they know what is a hit today and what was a hit yesterday. Quite often they are willing to take a chance on a song that reminds them of a current or recent hit, while they won't take a chance on something that is revolutionary or unusual—the potential hits of tomorrow.

It seems unjust when songwriters strive so hard to be original only to find, sometimes, that that very originality is keeping them from connecting in a commercial way. There is a romantic notion of a publisher dropping all commercial concerns when a song of great artistic quality passes over his desk. But music publishing is a business, and unless a publisher can get his songs recorded, a publisher's business will go under. So while the songwriter has artistic and aesthetic concerns, the publisher necessarily must have commercial concerns, so as to keep his business alive.

Therefore, the songwriter has to play the publisher's game. You have to present your song, first of all, in a form that the publisher can easily understand. This means a demo of no more than three songs.

▼ *Won't a publisher be impressed with me as a writer if I show him how many great songs I've written?*

No. Understand that in addition to your tape, a publisher probably has about fifty others on his desk, asking to be listened to. When he sees your tape come along containing twenty songs, he won't be impressed, he'll be put off. Knowing he doesn't have time to listen to all twenty, chances are he won't listen to any of them, figuring that any songwriter foolish enough to send that many songs isn't professional enough to deserve his attention in the first place.

I've made this same mistake. Wanting to impress publishers with my prolificacy, I have sent tapes of twenty-plus songs. And not a single publisher was interested. The actual effect seemed to be to diminish the value of each song. Because if you've got twenty all thrown together on a tape, how much is one of them going to be worth? But if you have only one song on a tape, or maybe two, you can be sure that those songs will receive more attention.

One publisher even wrote back to me to say, "Never send more than three songs. It's against all the rules." Dismayed by his lack of imagination, I foolishly wrote back "There are no rules, only people boring enough to play by them." Needless to say, that kind of approach wasn't in my best interest and led to no recordings of my songs. In time you learn that the competition is so great among songwriters, and publishers are so unwilling to take any risk, that unless you conform somewhat and play by the rules, you won't even have a chance of staying in the game.

So if you have twenty great songs, wonderful! Make good recordings of every one of them and target them for certain publishers.

▼ *What is targeting?*

Doing your homework and learning what kind of material each publisher is looking for. There are publishers who are looking for R&B, publishers looking for country, publishers looking for pop, etc. Find out what kind of material they are looking for, and target your songs directly for that market.

Targeting, or "casting," also refers to deciding

on a particular artist for one of your songs and finding out how to get a song to that artist. For example, if you target a song for Dolly Parton, you can call her record company or her manager to see if there is any way of getting material to her.

Talk to other songwriters and people in songwriter associations to find out which publishers are most open to new material. While there are many who might be willing to meet with you and listen to new songs, how many of them will have any intention of holding onto anything? Do some research to find out which publishers have recently accepted new material from new writers.

▼ Is it a good idea to get tip sheets?

Some people claim that all tip sheets are a waste of time and money while others swear by their use. Tip sheets are compilations of listings of publishers looking for specific kinds of material. For example, if you are a member of the National Academy of Songwriters, you will receive each issue of *SongTalk* magazine in which there is an insert called "Open Ears" that is such a tip sheet, listing publishers or producers looking for specific kinds of songs.

There are many other tip sheets available for songwriters:

Parade of Stars, Nashville (615) 320-7287

Song Placement Guide, L.A. (213) 285-3661

Song Connection, L.A. County (818) 763-1039

New on the Charts, New York (212) 921-0165 (This is available only to published songwriters.)

The most valuable asset of using a tip sheet is that you are not starting cold, blindly calling publishers without any sense of who is currently looking for material. Publishers (and producers) go through periods of actively looking for songs, and periods of working the songs they have found. Tip sheets enable you to get to a publisher at the right time—when he's open to new material—and with a knowledge of what kind of material is required.

Without the benefit of tip sheets, you have the task before you of calling up numerous publishers and asking, over the phone, "Are you currently accepting material?" And you will find that the majority of publishers you call will not be accepting

material, as they are already swamped with song demos. So by using a tip sheet, not only are you taking a shortcut straight to the source, but you are impressing on the publisher that you're in the know and on the inside of this game. Publishers want to work with pros, and you are only as professional as you present yourself.

Keep in mind that it takes a lot of time to compile tip sheets so that by the time they reach you, they might already be dated. If you do want to get them, be prepared to act fast.

Some tip sheets are exclusive and won't let beginners subscribe. They do this to maintain a high level of professionalism on their submissions.

▼ If a publisher says, "No, we are not now accepting outside material," should I cross him off my list?

No. Anytime that you hear that response: "We are not now accepting outside material," your immediate next question should be "When will you be accepting material?" Then mark down the response and the date and keep an organized, clear record of when you first called, and when they told you they would accept material. If they won't tell you exactly when to call back, call back in exactly two weeks and repeat the process, continuing to do so until they relent and let you submit something.

If they say that they will accept material in a month, make sure you make a careful note of that and contact them in exactly a month, explaining that you are following instructions.

Persistence is the name of the game. One well-known L.A. music publisher told us how she uses this exact process on her end to weed out the hobbyists from the persistent professionals. When anybody calls her office asking if she is accepting new material, she, or one of her assistants, will always answer, "Not now, but we will be accepting material in a month." Then, and only then, if a person calls back a month later saying, "You told me to call in a month," she will make an appointment to meet with them and listen to their songs.

The reason she goes this route is because it gives her some basic information about the writer: it shows that he is organized to the point of following up on the initial call and keeping a record of his calls, it shows that he has the ambition necessary to fuel a career in this competitive business, and it shows that he has the persistence and faith in himself to wait a full month and call back, rather than to give up. All in all, it shows that the writer is a professional. She said you'd be surprised by how few writers actually fall into this category. Most of them hear one "no" as in, "No, we are not accepting material at this moment," and give up.

So if you are now at the stage where you feel ready to market your songs, get organized. If you have a computer, you can use it to keep records: keep copies in the computer or on file of all correspondence and the dates letters were mailed; keep a list with dates of all calls you make to publishers and the replies you receive. If they tell you, as in our previous example, to call back in a month, keep an accurate record of that and call back in a month.

If you don't have a computer, all of this record keeping can be done in a journal or a notebook. Make sure you keep it all together. There's so much paperwork already involved in the art and craft of songwriting that you don't need any more, so if you can keep it in one place it will make the process simpler.

▼ Isn't a rejection of a song by a publisher a pretty good sign that a song isn't good?

Not necessarily. There are thousands of reasons why a publisher might not like a song on any particular day. He might be having a bad day or be in a bad mood for some reason. It might remind him of a song he has had no luck placing. He might simply not like the song based on his personal taste; another publisher might love it. Many great songs were rejected countless times before one publisher took a chance, and launched a hit.

Publishers are often looking for very specific material at any particular time. A publisher looking for a ballad for Judy Collins is not going to accept any song that doesn't fit into that slot; if he rejects your rocker, it doesn't mean that it's not good, only that he didn't want to pitch it to Judy Collins.

There are countless examples of classic songs that were initially rejected, sometimes repeatedly, by publishers before getting that one shot which led to success, proving that rejection by a publisher in no way means that a song isn't good. As Ray Evans of Livingston & Evans told us, "Every hit we had was turned down all over the place. 'Mona Lisa' was not going to even be released. Nat Cole said, 'Who wants this? Nobody will ever buy this.' 'To Each His Own' was laughed at. They said, 'Who wants a song with that title?' "

"To Each His Own," the song that was laughed at, had not one but *five* versions recorded of it in the Top Ten in August of 1947: 1, Eddie Howard; 3, Tony Martin; 5, Freddie Howard; 7, the Modernaires; and 8, The Inkspots. Not too shabby for a song that was initially laughed at by a publisher.

Understand that publishers are in this business to make money, not to support the arts. Therefore, they are much more likely to become enthused about a song if it currently fits into some commercial slot, so that they will have an easy time getting it placed. You could come in with a potential masterpiece, say "Strawberry Fields Forever," and have no luck whatsoever in getting it published. The reason is because it is too artistic and unusual for other artists—with the exception of John Lennon—to record. Notice how many times "Strawberry Fields" has been covered? Hardly any. But many of the Beatles' other songs, such as "Yesterday" and "Michelle" have been covered thousands of times, because those songs are more conventional, both musically and lyrically.

To gain any kind of success as a songwriter, you have to learn to take all rejections in stride, understanding that every great songwriter has been rejected countless times, and also that a rejection is much more a business judgment than an artistic judgment. The main thing that will keep you from success as a songwriter is your own giving up. If you're the type of person that can't withstand rejection, you're in the wrong business. But those songwriters who never give up and persist beyond all odds are the ones who will ultimately succeed.

▼ Once I get through to a publisher, then what happens?

A couple things can happen. Here's some possibilities:

1. The publisher wants to hold your song. He doesn't offer you a contract; he simply agrees to hold the song for a certain period of time so that

he can test it out. During that time, he will try to place the song and if he has success, then he will sign a contract with you in which you agree that he will serve as the exclusive publisher of the song for a period of time, during which you cannot pitch the song elsewhere.

2. The publisher will sign an exclusive one-song contract with you immediately, rather than hold the song first. This means that you can't take the song elsewhere.

3. The publisher will sign a nonexclusive, one-song contract, meaning that he has the rights to try and place the song but that the writer is still free to pitch the song elsewhere during this period.

▼ While he is holding the song, can I take it to another publisher?

That depends on your agreement with the publisher. If you sign an exclusive contract for the song that gives him exclusive rights to publishing the song, you cannot take it elsewhere. If you sign a nonexclusive, single-song contract, the publisher only has rights to the song if he gets it placed, but the songwriter is still free to shop the song on his own until that time.

There are also many cases in which there is no contract at all, but the publisher wants to try to place the song. Rather than put anything into writing, a publisher might say, "Let me try to work this song for a few days and see what I can do with it." Accepting this offer is up to the songwriter, but before making any decisions, he should be sure that he is dealing with a reputable publisher who has a decent track record. Taking the song elsewhere during this process might cause bad faith between you and the publisher, so if he is in a good position to help your career, let him hold on to it for a while.

▼ Is a song published once we sign a contract?

No. A song is not considered actually *published* until it is recorded and released for distribution. The contract details the percentages the publisher and writer will receive when and if a song is pub-

lished, and it gives the publisher the exclusive rights to a song.

▼ What should a songwriter look for in a single-song contract?

The National Academy of Songwriters offers a list of points to remember when negotiating a single-song contract with a publisher.

1. **A Reversion Clause for Nonpublication:** In the event that a commercial recording of your song is not released within a year (this period could be shorter: six months, or longer; two years), all rights should revert to the songwriter automatically. You may wish to impose other qualifications on the release (such as the name of an artist, or an artist with a Top-20 release within the last two years).

[A reversion clause will set a time period during which the publisher can work the song, after which all of the rights to the song will revert to the writer. In effect it's like putting the song on hold for a year or half-year during which the publishers, hopefully, will do their damnedest to get it placed.

It's recommended to get a six-month reversion clause if you can, and certainly no longer than a one-year reversion clause. A good publisher should be able to do something with your song within six months. If a full year goes by with no action on the song, either the publisher or the song is ineffective and it's in your best interest to move on. If the song is good, it will serve you best to get it back from the publisher who can't get it recorded and get it to one who can.

If, however, the publisher *is* able to place the song within the prescribed period of time, that reversion is canceled and the publisher retains the publishing rights to the song.]

2. **Mechanical Royalties:** A publisher may not grant a mechanical license for less than the statutory rate to any affiliated record company without writer consent.

[This makes sure that the writer does not get a lower rate of mechanical royalties than what is standard.]

3. **Payment of Royalties:** Writer's royalties should be paid within thirty days, no more than

ninety days, after the calendar half-year. The statements should show activities in reasonable detail, and the writer should have the right to audit the publisher to verify royalty statements rendered.

[This secures that the writer will receive his royalties within a reasonable amount of time and will have the option of reviewing the publisher's business records to make sure he is being paid accurately.]

4. **Changes in Words or Music:** No changes should be made without giving the writer first opportunity.

5. **Advances:** The writer should ask for an advance for the song; however, not all publishers will give them.

6. **Demo Costs:** The publisher should either absorb the costs of making demos or split such costs fifty-fifty with the writer.

7. **Unspecified Use:** The writer should be paid 50 percent of monies the publisher receives for "any and all other uses of the composition" not otherwise specifically provided for in the contract.

[This means that if the song is used for any other purposes, such as in a commercial, that the writer receives half of the income that endeavor generates.]

8. **No Cross-Collateralization:** Royalty advances and expenses should be charged against only that particular song; not against royalties from any other song the publisher may own.

[This protects the songwriter from imaginative bookkeeping, in which royalties from separate songs get intermixed. This keeps each song separate.]

9. **Withholding of Royalties:** If the publisher withholds writers' royalties due to a claim against the publisher regarding the song, the amount should be reasonably related to the amount of the claim. The writer should have the right to post a bond to recover withheld royalties. If money is recovered in a suit, the writer should receive 50 percent.

[This means that if there is any suit against the song then a publisher cannot retain all of your royalties from all of your songs to deal with that claim. The amount of money the publisher does

withhold has to be decided according to the amount specified in the suit. And if any money is received by the publisher in the suit, the songwriter receives half.]

10. **Assignment of the Contract:** The writer should be advised of such assignment.

11. **Payments:** No monetary payments should be made to the publisher for services rendered.

▼ *Do publishers usually give advances to songwriters for songs? Do they provide money for demos?*

Time was when a publisher would give advances to writers to encourage them and enable them to support themselves while churning out hit songs. Nowadays, unfortunately, receiving an advance from a publisher—especially for a beginning songwriter with little or no track record—is next to impossible. The business has shifted and the songwriter ultimately suffers because of it. Today there is such an abundance of songwriters competing who provide publishers with a torrent of materials that it's not in the publisher's best economic interest to lend the fledgling songwriter any monetary support.

Similarly, publishers take advantage of the fact that there is such a glut of available talent that they rarely will provide money for demos. They expect songwriters to not only fund their own demo projects, but provide them with fully produced, completely realized demos of the songs.

Van Dyke Parks, Warner Brothers' recording artist and cowriter with Brian Wilson of many of the Beach Boys' songs, including the classic "Heroes and Villains," objected to this system when he told *SongTalk*: "This is an industry in which you have to show all of your moves and give a full-fledged demonstration of a song before it gets recorded. A songwriter's not allowed to be poor these days."

▼ *Isn't it possible that this reliance on songwriters to have money as well as talent will eventually diminish the available source of artistry?*

Indeed. Publishers, as well as record company executives, seem to share the feeling that there is an unlimited source of talent and that if one songwriter is discouraged, there are at least a thousand others ready and willing to take his place. Making it in the music business as a songwriter is harder today than it has ever been due to this kind of thinking, as well as to the fact that so many of today's recording artists are self-contained "vertical artists" who write their own songs and have no need for outside material. For this reason, the odds against succeeding as a songwriter are stacked against you. Only those with powerful determination and a feeling that they will never give up, no matter what, will have the chance to succeed.

Mike Greene, current president of the National Academy of Recording Arts & Sciences (NARAS, the organization that presents the Grammy Awards) discussed this and other issues in *Song-Talk*: "We've got a huge task before us to reorient our society to the importance of art and culture . . . in our small way, and in the National Academy of Songwriter's small way, that's what we do. Our music people, God love them, are totally ignored. They are forgotten by almost everybody. When you are dealing with the protection of intellectual properties, thank God there are a few people who make money off of them so that they can lobby on behalf of the songwriters who are working day gigs. And that's where most of them are. Working at department stores or setting up microphones in a studio or doing other things so that they can do what they love. . . . We can't give up one inch of ground. If you give up one inch of ground, you've just lost ten thousand music people. And then we don't have a choice. It gets back to the talent pool principle. Filling that pool and making it bigger makes music better. We have to keep using every opportunity to keep driving these points home to people who never think about them."

Greene's points should be well taken. If you want to make it as a songwriter these days, you might have to first find a way to support yourself that is separate from songwriting. If you can find a job that does involve music, however, all the better.

Greene mentioned those songwriters working in recording studios moving mikes around, and this is an ideal job for beginning songwriters. I worked as a "second engineer" (also known as gopher) at a 24-track recording studio when I first

moved to Hollywood, and this was an excellent place to be for a number of reasons. It provided some financial support (though not much) while it was also a wonderful education: not only did I become familiar with every kind of microphone and piece of outboard gear available, I also saw firsthand what works and what fails in recording approaches. And one of the best payoffs was that I was able to use the studio myself—for my own recording and band rehearsals—in downtime, when the studio was unbooked.

To get this job, I got a list of every recording studio in Los Angeles, and began calling them. The name of the studio that hired me started with a "B," so I didn't even have to go beyond the first page of my list.

Todd Rundgren, songwriter and producer extraordinaire, also encouraged songwriters to get a music-related job to support the songwriting. Todd began his own career as an engineer, enabling him to write the songs he wants to and still have a viable way of making a living. As he told *SongTalk*, "I would say don't attempt to make a living and consider yourself an artist at the same time. If someone wants to be an artist, then get a job that pays and you can depend on and don't be any less devoted to your artistry and hope at some point it will happen for you. . . . You've got to decide, 'If I'm going to be a songwriter, I'm going to have to devote myself to that craft . . . and not depend on making a living on it.' "

One of Todd Rundgren's most beautiful songs (from *A Capella*) is called "Something To Fall Back On." And that's what we're talking about here, having something to fall back on until your songwriting career can support you.

▼ *What is a staff writer?*

A staff writer is a songwriter who gets a job with a publishing company writing songs exclusively for them. Nowadays with so many writers working independently, many publishing houses don't employ staff writers anymore, though a number of them continue to do so.

There are pros and cons with staff writing. The pros include not having to search out a publisher for each song; you have one built in. You also have a good chance of getting many songs placed, as you are on the inside as a staff writer, knowing immediately when a certain artist needs a certain kind of song. And since the publisher has made a financial investment in you, it's in his best interest to get your songs cut. Many producers will go directly to major publishers when needing material, and the publisher will choose songs from their existing catalog or assign a project to a staff writer. The staff writer, then, has excellent inside access to the pop machine.

The cons include having to write songs in a nine-to-five manner, coming in every day and doing your job of writing songs, something that can turn songwriting into drudgery. Of course, countless incredible songs have been written precisely this way. Lamont Dozier remembers working at Motown being like working at a factory, where you come in every day and punch the clock. Yet the songs that emerged from this process are some of the most enduring ones to have been written in the last few decades, including "You Keep Me Hanging On," "Stop in the Name of Love," "Reach Out— I'll be There," and so many others too numerous to mention. The same was true for those writers in and around the Brill Building in New York in the sixties, such as Mann & Weil and Goffin & King. For some writers, it seems as if staff writing forces them to make songwriting a job, and gives them the discipline to work on it every day that they might not have on their own. It's one thing to complain about never having enough time to write. It's another thing altogether to have unlimited time to write and actually use that time in a constructive way.

▼ If the songwriter writes the song and the publisher publishes the song, who owns it? Who makes the money on it?

The rights to a song get split in half: half of the rights—and the royalties generated by a song—are the songwriter's and half are the publisher's.

Although they both do make money from the song, it's the publisher and not the writer who controls the rights of the songs and who can make decisions as to how the song will be used.

▼ Wouldn't it make more sense to keep your own publishing, because you would make twice as much money?

Not necessarily. An established music publisher has an advantage over a beginning songwriter because he is entrenched in the business and has the connections necessary to get songs recorded. It is no easy feat these days to even get a song to a producer or an artist, let alone convince them to record one. A publisher with a track record, though, has access to the right people because he has provided good material in the past. So a beginning songwriter would almost always be in far better shape allowing a good publisher who wants your song to have half of the royalties so that he can get a good cut for you. Half of something is always better than all of nothing.

For this reason it's also advisable to do your homework and find out which publishers have a good track record and which ones have been striking out. It won't do you any good to have your song tied up for a year with a publisher who can't get it recorded. I know, from having had some of my best songs out of circulation for a whole year in a publisher's office where they did little more than collect dust.

Many producers will immediately go to the large publishing firms when they need new material for their artists, and staff writers or writers represented by those companies will get the majority of all cuts on albums. So it is in your best interest to get your songs to the best publishers, the ones who are having the most current success. If you can get the attention of a major publisher, you are in good shape. If you can't, it's best to understand your competition and realize that your songs might not get the same chance of success that they would with a more prominent publisher.

▼ Are there any advantages to being your own publisher?

Yes. A songwriter might have little other choice than to self-publish if he is unable to garner much interest in his work among established publishers. Instead of putting additional energy into getting publishers interested in his songs, he can put that energy into getting songs directly to artists and the representatives of artists, the job of the publisher.

There are other reasons why self-publishing can be beneficial. If you do get a self-published song recorded, you will make more money on it than if you do not own the publishing portion of the song's income. You can also control which songs of yours will get pitched. If you are pitching songs to publishers, it's up to them which songs of yours they will accept, and to whom they will pitch those songs. As your own publisher, you can personally decide if a song of your's should be directed towards a specific artist. You avoid the middleman, the music publisher, and pitch songs yourself.

For example, if you have a song that a publisher might consider "too wacky" or unusual to be interested in, yet you feel instinctually that you can hear a certain artist sing it, you can skip what can be an exercise in futility—attempting to convince a publisher of a song's worth—and pitch the song directly to the artist or producer yourself. As a musician yourself, it may well be that your instincts line up more closely to that artist's than do the business instincts of a music publisher.

You can also work harder to get a certain song recorded than would the average music publisher, who is working many songs by many writers. As a self-published writer, you can devote an entire month or more to attempting to place a single song. Whereas a music publisher might give up on a song after a single pitch to a specific producer, you could try every route imaginable: getting the song to the artist's manager's secretary with a bunch of roses; getting it to the producer's assistant, the producer's niece, the manager's second cousin's best friend, etc. Take it up every possible path, and your chances of success are far greater than giving it only one shot.

Publishers, producers, and artists have all expressed that the songs they finally listened to were the ones most aggressively or imaginatively delivered. If you go to some outlandish means—keeping in mind not to break the law—to get a song to somebody, chances are you *will* make an impression. Of course, if you haven't got the goods to begin with, none of this will help. But if you have a great song, a song you truly believe in, by publishing it yourself you can do whatever it takes to get it heard by the right people.

▼ How does one establish a publishing company?

It's not too hard, as unlike most other businesses, you can do it right out of your home without opening an office. As stated earlier, you don't have to get a special license to be a music publisher nor do you need any minimum of education (though some songwriters think a little musical education wouldn't be bad for some publishers). Both ASCAP and BMI are obligated to accept as a publisher member any person who is getting songs recorded and distributed. BMI has a twenty-five dollar application fee to be a publisher. ASCAP has an annual fee of fifty dollars to be a publisher member. (See the next section on Business for more information on BMI and ASCAP.)

To be a publisher, you have to choose a name for your company, and in some parts of the country you will have to run what is called a fictitious business name statement to make that name official. To find out what is required of you, call the office of the Secretary of State in your state. You also have to join one of the performance rights' organizations—ASCAP, BMI, or SESAC—as a publisher member. When you do that, they will run a worldwide search on the name of your company to make sure no other publisher is using the same name. Naturally, if you are already a writer member of one of these organizations, that is the one to join as a publisher. You can seek advice from their representatives about how best to get started as a publisher. It's also advisable to consult a lawyer when starting your own company, just as you would when starting any new business.

The next step is to open a new bank account for your company. All monies earned or spent by the company should come from this account, and should be kept separate from all other accounts.

Get stationery and cards that identify your company. If you can, get a logo designed that people will begin to identify with your company, and have this printed on tape labels as well. If you have a computer with graphic capabilities, you can do all of this yourself.

Send out a press release to local papers and magazines as well as to record companies and producers to notify them that a new publishing company has been established to represent your songs.

A songwriter who publishes his own material rarely prints sheet music of his songs but can make a deal with independent music printers to do that for him as well as to set up a distribution system for the printed music.

▼ ────────────────────────

Songwriter Options.

1. Single-song contract, nonexclusive.
   This is a contract that gives a publisher non-exclusive rights to a song, meaning that the songwriter is free to shop the song elsewhere during the period of time that the contract is in effect. If the songwriter places the song himself during the period specified in the contract, the publisher relinquishes all rights to the song. This kind of contract allows the songwriter to take the song to more than one publisher at a time.

   Why would a publisher sign this kind of contract? Basically out of a sense of fairness to the songwriter. They figure that if they can't place the song, the songwriter should have the freedom to try to place the song himself.

2. Exclusive Single-Song Contract.
   This is a contract in which the songwriter is granting exclusive rights for a single song to a publisher for a prescribed period of time. With this contract, the songwriter *is not free* to shop the song to other publishers. And even if the songwriter somehow secures a recording of the song, the publisher would still receive 50 percent of the song's income. The songwriter should only sign this kind of contract with a reputable publisher (one with a good track record showing that he has what it takes to get the song placed) and with a firm reversion clause (six months is a perfect period of time for this; it should definitely be no longer than one year).

3. Exclusive (multi-song) Songwriter Contract.
   This is a contract in which the songwriter grants exclusive rights to a publisher for not one song but for all the songs the writer creates during a specified period of time. Under this contract the songwriter is obliged to render all songs that he writes exclusively to the publisher for a prescribed time period. This is similar but not the same as a staff-writer position in which you are an employee of a publishing company.

   With this contract a publisher can retain the rights to all the songs an artist writes for his own album; it's a publishing contract that parallels a recording contract.

   It's customary when signing this kind of contract to receive an advance against future royalties. It's also common for the publisher to have an option to extend the terms of the agreement, though this clause is usually contingent on the publisher's ability to place that writer's material with other artists, or to seek other uses for the songs such as in films and TV programs.

4. Self-publishing.
   This is when a songwriter serves as his own publisher, publishing and working to place his own material. A songwriter is the sole owner of a song's copyright from the moment the song is first created. The songwriter is under no obligation to split his rights to a song with any publisher and can always retain publishing. However, without the help of an established publisher it can be difficult to impossible to get your songs recorded.

   If you're a songwriter recording your own albums and you have a record contract, the need for placing songs is not as great since your songs will be placed on your own album. If so, owning your own publishing business can be quite beneficial as you won't have to split any of your publishing royalties. Prince, for example, doesn't have to worry about making sure that other artists record his material because he can record his songs and have hits with them by himself, and so his income isn't solely dependent on getting his songs placed. For him self-publishing could be a good idea since he is ensured that a good number of his songs will be recorded each year.

   However, Prince can generate additional income as well as spreading the gift of his music further by having his songs cut by other artists. I'm sure he hasn't minded having his songs recorded by everyone from Sheena Easton to Tom Jones. Having a recording contract means that these artists will have an opportunity to hear his songs for themselves, something a nonrecording songwriter does not have.

A nonperforming songwriter's entire livelihood is reliant upon getting her songs recorded by artists and so has much greater need for a publisher than a singer/songwriter. Without a built-in system of having your songs heard, getting cuts on your own without a publisher can be quite difficult, especially when trying to give time to your songwriting.

5. Copublishing.

This is when the writer retains a portion of the publisher's share of the song's royalties. In most copublishing situations, the publisher retains control of the song's copyright and the writer exercises no control over the *use* of the song; he is only an income participant.

6. Administration Deals.

In an administration deal, the songwriter hires a person—perhaps an attorney—to do the administration for a song or a catalog of songs but not to control or own the songs. This basically refers to doing the paper work: issuing licenses, administrating the collection of royalties for a song, and keeping the records. The songwriter in this situation retains the right to control the use of the song.

For example, Steinberg & Kelly, the team that wrote "Like a Virgin" and "True Colors" explained at a *SongTalk* seminar that they represent their songs themselves rather than having a publishing deal and they have a lawyer who administrates their catalog. This allows them the freedom to pitch their songs themselves (something they are in a position to do after having proven themselves as a hitmaking team) while still being secure in the knowledge that their catalog of songs is being well tended to.

▲

Music Business

▼ What is a pitch?

A pitch is an attempt to get a song published or recorded. You can pitch a song to a record company, a publisher, or directly to an artist.

Even those writers with an outstanding, proven track record, still have to sell their own songs. And like a salesman, you've got to sell that publisher on not only the song, but on you as the writer.

As Lamont Dozier told *SongTalk*: "Writing the songs is the most important thing. But you do have to be aware very much of what is happening businesswise. You have to be where all the happenings are happening. You have to do whatever it takes, outside of breaking the law, to get your songs to people.

"It doesn't get easier," Lamont continued, "over the years to blow your own horn. It's a constant uphill climb. Because you're always auditioning.

"You can go to song-pluggers and pay them and then wait around for the phone to ring to see if they've got anything going. By that time you can go stark-raving mad. You can do the same thing they do yourself."

▼ Should a songwriter ever try to pitch songs directly to an artist? And how do you get to an artist? Does it make sense to go through an artist's manager?

Songwriters should try every possible route that they can find to get their songs placed. If you

have access to an artist, by all means, use it! Getting a song directly to a recording artist means skipping over many of the middlemen and going straight to the source.

Of course, it's not always easy to get directly to an artist, and songs mailed to artists will rarely meet their destinations. Going through a manager, or even a manager's assistant, secretary, or second cousin, is a viable approach. Basically, do everything you can to get your song to the right person. Leave no stone unturned.

▼ Why won't an artist listen to a song if it's mailed to them?

Because of the many song-plagiarism cases that have taken place lately. Simply by opening an envelope that contains your tape in it, an artist is opening himself up to a potential lawsuit. Even if there is no actual resemblance between your song and one of their's, they are vulnerable for the rest of their lives to a lawsuit claiming one of their songs—even one written fifteen years from now—is stolen from that song you sent them in the mail. For this reason, artists, as well as many producers, managers, record company executives, and even most publishers, will not listen to tapes that are "unsolicited."

▼ What is meant by "unsolicited"?

Unsolicited refers to any tape that is sent cold, without permission. Permission must be asked for and received to send a tape before a tape is considered "solicited."

Record companies, artists, producers, and others will accept tapes that come from representatives with whom they are familiar but not from songwriters with whom they are not familiar.

▼ Does it make sense for a songwriter to have an attorney?

Yes, it does. In time, you will need an attorney to review contracts and other legal matters. And if you are a "vertical" artist who wants to get a record deal, it is difficult to even get a record company artists and repertoire (A&R) person to listen to a tape. Nowadays the usual way of getting a record contract is by hiring an attorney to "shop your tape" to various companies. If your tape comes in to a company represented by an attorney who is known in the business, you will be taken seriously.

▼ What is a catalog?

A writer's catalog is the sum total of all the songs he has written (and has preserved in a fixed form) or all the songs owned by a publishing company. Not every writer owns his own catalog, though, strangely enough. For example, Michael Jackson owns the Beatles' catalog because he bought ATV Music, which owned the publishing rights to all of the Beatles' songs (except for a very few).

▼ What is a copyright?

A copyright is the exclusive right to reproduce, publish, and sell the matter and form of a literary, musical, or artistic work.

A song is actually a literary *and* a musical work as it is comprised of both words and music.

In simpler terms, a copyright is a form of protection for a creative work which is provided by the United States of America under Title 17 of the U.S. Code. This protection proves authorship of the creative work.

▼ How do I get a copyright for my song?

Technically, your song is copyrighted as soon as you complete it and put it in some kind of a fixed form. This fixed form can be a musical transcription of the song with the lyrics in place. It can also be a recording of the song on tape or disc.

To *register* a copyright is different from attaining a copyright. You attain a copyright as soon as you put your song into a fixed form. Registering a copyright does not give you any more protection for a song; it's a way of establishing a public record of your claim of authorship and the date of creation. Though registration is not required and will not provide additional protection for your song, it is encouraged.

Registration will establish solid evidence of ownership and validity of your copyright if it is made within five years of the publication of the song.

Registration will insure the receipt of any licensing fees pertaining to your songs. This means that if the song gets used in a movie, for example, you will be insured, as the registered writer, to receive whatever money is generated.

▼ How much does it cost to get a copyright?

Nothing. Again, a copyright goes into effect at the instant that a work is put into a fixed form, either a "copy" or a "phonorecord." To *register* a copyright, however, does cost money; ten dollars per song as of this writing.

▼ How long after copyrighting a song can I register it?

There is no time limit. You can register a copyright at any time.

▼ How do I register a copyright?

To register a copyright, you are required to deposit "copies" or "phonorecords" of the work with the Library of Congress in Washington, D.C. You must fill out Form PA from the Copyright office (PA stands for Performing Arts).

If your purpose is to register a copyright for a sound recording—not the song itself but the recording—you need to fill out an application known as Form SR (SR stands for Sound Recording). Form SR should be used when the copyright is limited to the sound recording itself.

You can attain either of these forms by calling the Library of Congress in Washington, D.C. at any of the following numbers:

Public Information (202) 479-0700

Forms and Circular Hotline (202) 707-9100

Reference and Bibliography Section (202) 707-6787

Copyright General Counsel's Office (202)707-8380

Documents Unit (202) 707-1759

Licensing Division (202) 707-8150

▼ ─────────────────────────────

To register a copyright, you must send to the Library of Congress in Washington, D.C.:

1. Two copies or phonorecords of the work
2. A Form PA
3. A check or money order for ten dollars

───────────────────────────── ▲

▼ What's the difference between a "copy" and "phonorecord"?

A "copy" refers to "objects from which a work can be read or visually perceived, directly or with the aid of a machine or a device, such as manuscripts, sheet music, film, or videotape." This does not refer to tapes or records of a song which are known as "phonorecords."

A "phonorecord" is an object "embodying fixations of sounds, such as tapes and phonograph disks, commonly known as phonograph records."

Therefore, a song can be registered as a "copy" that refers to sheet music, or as a "phonorecord" that refers to a tape or record of the song.

▼ Will a sound recording copyright (Form SR) protect the copyright of my song as well?

No. The sound recording copyright, which you can only get by filling out Form SR, only pertains to the protection of the sounds on the record, and whoever owns the recording—usually the record company—owns the sound recording copyright. The writer needs a song copyright to protect the song itself; register this by filling out Form PA.

▼ What is meant on the PA form by "Nature Of This Work"? If it's a song should I just write "song"?

Since you can register a copyright for other works besides songs, this is the place where you specify the type of work you are registering. For example, besides songs you can register a play, a movie, and even pantomime or choreography (if they are in a fixed form).

You can also register a song lyric without music, and a melody without lyrics. This is the place on the form where you specify what exactly you are registering.

If you are registering both the words and the music of a song, write "words and music." If you are registering only music without lyrics, write "music." If you are registering lyrics without music, write "song lyrics."

▼ Can you register for a new copyright on a song if it is a substantially rewritten version of a song that's already been registered?

Yes. And it is a good idea to do so as a changed song might be quite different from its original form.

To register a rewritten or changed song, you fill out the Form PA in the same manner but specify in Space Six on the form that the song is a "derivative work." All this means is that the song is derived from a previously existing work. Besides changes or revisions of a song, the term "derivative work" also includes musical arrangements, translations, or "any other form in which a work may be recast, transformed, or adapted."

▼ Is it possible to register a whole group of songs under one copyright?

Yes. You can register what is known as a "compilation" of songs. This is defined as "a work formed by the collection and assembling of preexisting materials or of data that are selected, coordinated, or arranged in such a way that the resulting work as a whole constitutes an original work of authorship."

To register a group of songs as a compilation,

you must group all of the songs together with a single title, such as "Smithsongs, 1989." Only this title will appear on the official records, not the separate title of each song. However, at the time that you do receive your copyright registration certificate for the collection, you can then list all of the individual titles on the Form CA (for an additional ten-dollar fee) to individually register your songs. Form CA is also utilized to correct errors on other registrations.

To file many songs under one title, all songs must be written by the same person or at least one person must have contributed as cowriter to all of the songs in the collection.

Unless your work was actually written to be a compilation of songs (a rock opera, for example) this is not a good method of protecting your individual songs. If any dispute over authorship does arise, your single song has no copyright protection and is protected only as one small part of the larger compilation, making it more difficult to prove authorship. It is recommended, therefore, that you register a copyright for each separate song.

▼ **Is it necessary to have your copyright registered before you can file any infringement suits in court?**

If registration is made prior to the publication of the song, or within three months after publication, attorney's fees and statutory damages will be available to the copyright owner in court actions. If registration is not made within these parameters, the copyright owner is subject only to receive awards based on actual damages and profits.

▼ **Does a song have to be published to get a copyright?**

No. The copyright protection is available both for published and nonpublished work.

▼ **What is the difference between the creation of a work and the publication of a work?**

Under the statute, a work is "created" when it is placed in a fixed form—either in a copy or a phonorecord.

A work is defined as being "published" when there is some distribution of copies or phonorecords to the public by sale or other transfer or ownership, or by "rental, lease, or lending." A work is also considered published if there has been an "offering to distribute copies or phonorecords to a group of persons for purposes of further distribution, public performance, or public display."

▼ *A publisher is holding two of my songs though he has yet to get them recorded. Should I consider these songs published?*

No. Until a publisher actually gets the songs recorded on a record that gets released (and is distributed to the public in some fashion), it is not a published work. Simply having a song "held" by a publisher is not the same as having the song published. (See page 79 for more information on publishing.)

▼ *I've heard that you have to send in a deposit when registering for a copyright. What kind of deposit is needed?*

The deposit in question is not a monetary one. It simply refers to copies or phonorecords that represent the work that is being registered. Registering is not a free service, however; it does cost you ten dollars per song.

If you are registering a single song that is unpublished, you must include a deposit of one complete copy or phonorecord of the song.

If you are registering a single song that is published, you must include a deposit of two complete copies or phonorecords of the best edition of the song.

If the song was first published outside of the United States, you must include a deposit of one complete copy or phonorecord of the first foreign edition.

If you are registering a contribution to a collective work, you must include a deposit of one complete copy or phonorecord of the best edition of the collective work.

▼ *Does my copyright have to be registered before I can use a copyright symbol on my song?*

No. You can use the notice of copyright, which is the copyright symbol (©) even before the copyright is registered.

The symbol is *required* only on what are called "visually perceptible copies" of your work. Audio tapes and records of a song are considered to be "phonorecords" and not copies and so do not require the copyright symbol. The copyright symbol is required on sheet music or lyric sheets containing your song.

Simply put the copyright symbol (©) or the word "Copyright" with the year of the first publication of the work (if unpublished, use the present year) and the name of the owner of the copyright.

▼ *Where should the copyright symbol be placed on my lyric sheets?*

The copyright symbol should be placed at the very bottom of the sheet with the year and the author's name. If the lyric sheet consists of more than one page, try to consolidate it! If you can't do so, place the symbol at the bottom of the final page.

Officially, the notice of a copyright should be affixed to the copies "in such a manner and location as to give reasonable notice of the claim of copyright."

▼ *How long does a copyright on a song last?*

The laws pertaining to copyrights were changed drastically as of January 1, 1978. Before that change, a copyright on a song lasted for a term of twenty-eight years from the date it was first secured, and a copyright was secured either on the day the song was published or on the date of registration if the song was registered prior to publication. The copyright became eligible for renewal during last year of the twenty-eight-year term. The new copyright law has extended that term from twenty-eight years to forty-seven years for any songs that had existing copyrights on January 1, 1978 (making a total seventy-five-year term). However, the copyright must be renewed for it to receive the total term.

Any song that is created in a fixed form on or after January 1, 1978, receives a different treatment from the Copyright Office under the new copyright laws. It is protected from the instant that it is put in a fixed form and lasts for the entire length of the songwriter's life plus an additional fifty years after the songwriter's death.

If more than one person writes a song, the copyright on the song will last of fifty years after the death of the last surviving collaborator.

▼ *How about if I wrote a song prior to 1978 but never registered it? How is it affected?*

Songs that were created before the present law receive automatic copyright protection and last as long as songs copyrighted since January 1, 1978: the life of the songwriter plus fifty years.

▼ *If I am hired to write a song, who owns the copyright?*

It belongs to the people who hire you. If a song is written "for hire," the copyright belongs to the employer, not the employee. If you are hired to write a song for a movie or TV show, the copyright belongs to the person or organization that hired you.

▼ *What is considered a "work for hire"?*

A "work for hire," according to the basic information that is given out with the PA form, is: (1) "a work prepared by an employee within the scope of his or her employment" or (2) "a work specially ordered or commissioned for use as a contribution to a collective work. . . . if the parties expressly agree in a written instrument signed by them that the work shall be considered a work made for hire."

If you indicate the work was made for hire, you must give the full legal name of the employer.

▼ *If I write a song with my collaborator, who owns the copyright?*

The writers of a song that is jointly written are both coowners of the copyright unless there is an agreement to the contrary.

▼ **If I come up with a great title before writing a song, can I copyright that title so it doesn't get stolen before I finish the song?**

No. Copyright protection is not available for titles and this is good for songwriters, as many great songs have been written with the same title.

Similarly, an *idea* for a song cannot be copyrighted no matter how original it might be. It's what you actually do with that idea, or that title, that matters in terms of copyright protection.

▼ **Is it possible to register a copyright for a song written by someone who is no longer alive?**

Yes. If the songwriter is deceased, you must include the writer's date of death on your application (unless the work is anonymous or pseudonymous). The birth date of the songwriter is optional but helpful.

▼ **What is meant by the terms "anonymous" and "pseudonymous" authorship?**

According to the information made available by the Copyright Office, a songwriter's work is considered "anonymous" if the songwriter's name is not identified on copies or records of the work. If the songwriter's name is a fictitious one (if you have a stage name, for example) the authorship is considered "pseudonymous."

▼ **How do I register a copyright for a song that has anonymous or pseudonymous authorship?**

If your song is "anonymous" you can do one of three things: leave the line where you fill in the author's name on the PA form blank; write "anonymous" on that line; or reveal the author's identity.

If your song is "pseudonymous" you also have three choices: leave the line blank; give the pseudonym and identify it as such (for example: "Walter Hemp, pseudonym"); or reveal the author's real name and identify the pseudonym (for example, "Tom Bowden, whose pseudonym is Tommy LeDome").

▼ **What is the NAS Songbank and can it be used instead of registering a copyright?**

The Songbank is one of many services offered to the members of the National Academy of Songwriters. It is a way of establishing ownership and date of creation of a song. It can also be used by nonmembers for a higher price. (As of this writing, the price of the Songbank is as follows: For member of NAS it is three dollars for the first song and seventy-five cents for each additional song registered at the same time. For nonmembers, it costs five dollars for the first song and three dollars for each additional song registered at the same time.)

The Songbank was started in 1973 by Helen King, the founder of NAS, who saw the need for songwriters to have a place where they could get immediate protection for their songs as a copyright registration can take up to six months to be finalized. She based the Songbank on a similar service for scripts offered by the Writer's Guild.

The Songbank is not meant to be a replacement for a registered copyright although it is solid proof of song authorship and will hold up in court if there is any dispute.

You can use the Songbank in person or by mail. It allows you to protect your song by putting a fixed form of it (either sheet music or a tape; a lyric sheet is optional unless, of course, you are registering only a lyric without music) in a documented envelope which is sealed by an employee of NAS and placed in a vault. The writer is given a copy of the document that serves as proof that your song is in the Songbank. Songs are kept in the Songbank for ten years, at which time the registration must be renewed.

If you cannot come in person to the NAS office in Hollywood, California, you can use the Songbank by mail by filling out a Songbank form that NAS will send you. Remember, being a member of NAS gives you a significant discount on the use of the Songbank so it is recommended.

▼ **What are performing rights?**

Performing rights are the rights granted under the U.S. Copyright Act to owners of musical works to perform a song in public. This includes all performances of the song on radio, TV, movies, concerts, restaurants, and clubs. Other people must pay you (in the form of performance royalties) for the right to perform your song in public.

▼ What are performance royalties?

These are the royalties collected by the performing rights organization when a song is performed, either over the airwaves or in live performance.

▼ What are performing rights organizations and what do they do?

They are the organizations set up to insure that songwriters receive all the money they have earned from performance royalties. These organizations are ASCAP, BMI, and SESAC. A professional songwriter must belong to one of them. Publishers do not pay writers any performance rights' money. That money is only paid to writers by one of the three performing rights organizations.

▼ Can you belong to both ASCAP and BMI?

No. You have to choose as it is not permitted for a writer or a publisher to collect fees on a song from more than one performing rights society.

▼ How do I choose which organization to belong to? Is there much of a difference between them?

There are some differences. ASCAP was founded in 1914 as a nonprofit organization that is owned by its members, who are both writers and publishers. It has approximately 26,500 writers and 11,000 publishers as members.

BMI was founded by the members of the National Association of Broadcasters (NAB) in 1940 when they could not come to an agreement with ASCAP on a new licensing contract. Although a new contract was eventually signed the next year, BMI remained and has since become a major performing rights society. It has approximately 65,000 writers and 65,000 publishers as members.

SESAC, (originally standing for the Society of European Stage Artists and Composers) was founded in 1931 by the Heinecke family and is still privately owned by them. For many years it served only music publishers, but in 1973 writers were allowed to join.

SESAC is the smallest of the three performing rights societies. According to SESAC itself, since it is smaller, it's able to be more selective in its affiliations with writers and publishers, and therefore is able to provide "efficient and personalized service" to every writer or publisher who belongs.

▼ Does SESAC represent different kinds of music than ASCAP and BMI?

In its early years, SESAC was primarily known for its representation of European classics, as well as religious and country music. Today, however, their affiliates are working in every style of music, from black/urban music to polka.

▼ Is there any fee required to join SESAC?

No. There is no fee required either for writers or publishers to join SESAC.

▼ Can any songwriter join SESAC?

No. To join SESAC you have to make an appointment to personally meet with a SESAC representative in their Affiliations Department, and then bring in a tape containing a maximum of three songs along with lyric sheets for each song. After the meeting, a music screening committee will evaluate your work and decide whether or not it is "mutually beneficial" for them to invite you to be an affiliate.

▼ Do you have to be a published writer to join BMI or ASCAP?

Yes, though you can join ASCAP as an associate writer. But until you have songs published, you will be earning no royalties and so do not have much need for ASCAP or BMI.

▼ How much does it cost to join ASCAP or BMI?

If you are a published songwriter, you can join ASCAP for a yearly membership of ten dollars that is deducted from whatever royalties you generate.

BMI has no membership fees for published songwriters (although it does cost a one-time twenty-five dollar fee for publishers to join).

▼ If I'm a published writer, is there any reason why ASCAP or BMI can refuse to allow me to join?

No. Under the United States consent decree, both ASCAP and BMI are obliged to accept as a member any writer who has had at least one song commercially published or recorded.

▼ How do ASCAP, BMI, and SESAC determine payment to writers?

They each have their own method of determining payment.

ASCAP collects payments by charging broadcasters a licensing fee to use their entire catalog. According to their literature, they license over 10,000 radio stations, 800 TV stations, and over 150,000 other music users including nightclubs, restaurants, retail stores, background music operators, concert promoters, symphony orchestras, colleges, and universities. The rate is just under 2 percent of a licensees' gross receipts. After deducting overhead, ASCAP then pays its writer-members and publisher-members an equal amount.

BMI, which was originally formed by broadcasters to compete with ASCAP, also charges a fee to broadcasters for use of its catalog, though it is a smaller amount than that charged by ASCAP.

▼ Don't ASCAP, BMI, or SESAC monitor all radio transmissions so that they know every single time my song gets played?

No. Only a small percentage of local radio broadcasts are sampled and then this report is multiplied according to statistical data. To monitor every radio station in the country would be logistically difficult, so logging is done in the same way polls and surveys are conducted: a small percentage represents the whole. For example, if five hundred stations are licensed and ten are logged during one period, that figure would be multiplied by fifty.

Both BMI and ASCAP do figure in the size and importance of a radio station, as well as the time of day a song is played, when compiling their logging data based on samples.

ASCAP claims to tape 60,000 hours of radio each year as well; these tapes are then sent to New York where they are analyzed.

Though BMI does not make tapes of radio programming, they claim to log many more stations than does ASCAP. They use the radio stations' own logs and playlists to determine what is aired.

The three TV networks do provide both ASCAP and BMI with detailed listings of all their programs and song usages on TV; ACSAP makes its own videotapes of TV shows to double-check the information provided by the networks.

BMI requires those broadcasters who purchase licenses to provide them, form time to time, a log that details music played within a certain period. A private accounting firm chooses which stations are to provide logs.

SESAC tracks the activity of a song by using data bases such as *Billboard*'s Information Network as well as checking radio playlists, TV music cue sheets, and popularity charts in *Billboard*, *Cash Box*, and *Radio & Records*.

▼ If they only log certain stations, how will they know if my song gets played on a station they don't log?

If your song is played on a major rock station in a major city, it is assumed that other rock stations in other cities would also be playing the song. So the number of times the song gets played on that one station that *is* logged would be multiplied by the number of similar stations around the country.

Naturally, since the societies do not log every single station in the country, it is quite possible to have your song receive airplay, and if this is never logged, you'll receive no royalties. One writer I know has written children's songs that have been receiving airplay recently on small local stations and college stations. But since none of these stations has been logged, she has received no royalties. It's not the most fair system, yet presently it is the best ASCAP and BMI can offer. However, there are various other methods of computer logging of music on radio and TV which are being developed and are stirring up some waves in the music industry. As computer technology makes logging easier, ASCAP and BMI's current methods will soon be outmoded; whether new systems will be accepted is yet to be seen.

▼ Do BMI and ASCAP license the use of music in Broadway shows?

No. The right to perform shows has to be obtained from the producer or publisher of the show (whoever owns or controls the copyright). This is what is known as "source licensing," which means that the work is licensed directly from the source, which in many cases can be the songwriter.

"Source licensing" is highly discouraged in other areas because it eliminates the songwriter's opportunity to earn any future royalties. A source license is a one-time fee.

Writers of these shows do collect payments on songs from the shows that are played elsewhere, as on TV or the radio.

▼ Do BMI and ASCAP monitor movies so that songwriters get royalties when their songs are used in films?

No. Like musical plays, the rights to music used in movies must be negotiated on a one-time-fee basis as the songwriter (or publisher) issues a synchronization license.

▼ If my song gets played on a jukebox, will I receive any royalties on it?

Yes. Prior to the copyright revisions of 1978 jukebox owners were not required to pay any licensing fees at all. As of the 1978 change, each jukebox owner was required to pay a fee of eight dollars for every jukebox. This has since been raised to a fee of fifty dollars for every jukebox.

▼ Will BMI, ASCAP, or SESAC help place my songs with publishers?

No. That's your job. Once the song is published, then the performing rights societies become involved.

▼ Will BMI, ASCAP, or SESAC promote my songs?

No. That's the job of the publisher.

▼ Will BMI, ASCAP, or SESAC give me legal advice?

No. They offer guidance but for legal advice you must go to a lawyer.

▼ Will BMI, ASCAP, or SESAC help me find a collaborator?

They can often help in this regard, though it is not a main function. To meet collaborators, I would suggest joining an organization such as the National Academy of Songwriters who provide the "Collaborator's Network" in their *SongTalk* newspaper.

▼ What happens if I'm a member of BMI and my collaborator belongs to ASCAP? Who collects and distributes the royalties?

Both. The member of BMI will receive payment form BMI, and the ASCAP member will receive payment form ASCAP. This is common; some of the world's most famous collaborators, such as Goffin and King, belong to different performing rights societies.

▼ Can I collaborate with a writer who does not belong to any performing rights society?

Sure. But until that writer does join one, he will not have any way of collecting his portion of your song royalties.

▼ Do ASCAP, BMI, or SESAC publish music or books?

No.

▼ Do they produce any records or tapes?

No.

▼ ─────────────────────────────────────

Where to find the performing rights societies

BMI has three main offices:

1. New York: 320 West 57th Street, New York, NY 10019 (212) 586-2000
2. Nashville: Music Square East, Nashville, TN 37203 (615) 259-3625
3. Los Angeles: 8730 Sunset Blvd., Hollywood, CA 90069 (213) 659-9109

BMI also has a toll-free number: 800-USA-BMI-1

ASCAP also has three main offices:

1. New York: 1 Lincoln Plaza, New York, NY 10023 (212) 870-7541
2. Nashville: 2 Music Square West, Nashville, TN 37203 (615) 244-3936
3. Los Angeles: 6430 Sunset Blvd., Hollywood, CA 90028 (213) 466-7681

SESAC has two main offices:

1. New York: 156 West 65th Street, New York, NY 10019 (212) 586-3450
2. Nashville: 55 Music Square East, Nashville, TN 37203 (615) 320-0055

SESAC has a toll-free line as well: 800-826-9996

─────────────────────────────────────▲

▼ Will my royalties from BMI or ASCAP include record sales?

No. ASCAP and BMI do not collect mechanical royalties on record sales. This is usually taken care of by your publisher or by your record company.

▼ What's the difference between a performance right and a mechanical right? And are there other kinds of rights I should know about?

A **mechanical right** is a right to reproduce a piece of music onto a record or a tape. These are the rights that allow a record company to use your song and they will pay the mechanical royalties.

A **performance right** is the right of the copyright owner to receive royalties when his song is performed in public, as we have already detailed.

These royalties go both to the writer and to the publisher.

Synchronization rights refer to when a piece of music is used on a soundtrack of a movie or TV show. To get synchronization rights, a TV or film producer must get what is called a "synch" license. Both mechanical royalties and synchronization fees are paid by TV and film producers and record companies directly to the owner of the copyright.

Most of the major American publishers are represented by the Harry Fox Agency, 205 East 42nd Street, New York, NY 10017 (212) 370-5330, which grants mechanical and synchronization licenses and collects fees on them.

▼ What are mechanical royalties?

These are the royalties generated by record sales and are paid by the record company to the publisher who pays a share to the songwriter.

▼ What is A&R?

A&R stands for Artists & Repertoire. It is the department of a record company that is responsible for finding artists, finding songs for artists, and developing artists. An A&R man or woman works in this department and is responsible for finding and developing talent.

▼ What is a "cut"?

A cut is a recording of a song. It also refers to a specific track on an album, as in "Check out the third cut—it's awesome!"

▼ What is a "cover"?

A cover is also a recording of a song, but it is usually a recording done after an original version of a song. For example, the first version of "Yesterday" was performed by the Beatles. All subsequent recordings or performances of it have been cover versions. The word is also used when a band or an artist performs their own original material, but also throws in a few covers, or songs by other artists. And bands that perform no original material, such and Top 40 bands, are also referred to as cover bands.

▼ *Is it necessary to perform to get a record deal? I've heard about some bands who have never performed and yet got a record deal based on great-sounding tapes.*

To get a record deal nowadays, it usually takes a lot more than great songs and a great-sounding demo. There have been examples of artists getting signed who have had no performing experience, but these are exceptions, mostly.

When an A&R person hears a tape he or she likes, their next step is not to sign up the artist. Understand that it takes upwards of fifty thousand dollars to launch a new artist. This is an enormous investment and not one record companies—or the A&R people whose jobs are on the line—take lightly. So if they hear a tape they like, they next discover if the band is gigging anywhere so that they can check out their live performance. And even if they enjoy the gig, unless there is some "buzz" about the band in town, some hype in the press, or a lot of word of mouth, the band or artist can remain unsigned. Record companies are often waiting for the public to support a band or artist before they will be brave enough to invest any of their own money.

To generate a buzz about a band or an artist, you need to play many gigs so that you can develop a following. And this isn't always easy because many of the gigs new bands land are on weekdays, like Wednesday night at eleven. And how many people are willing to turn out to see a new band late on a Wednesday night if they're not personal friends? And if they are personal friends, there are only so many times you can call on them before they're no longer friendly. So you have to walk that fine line of playing enough to develop a following, and not playing so much that people can easily pass up the gig, figuring they'll catch the next one.

And all of this means, unfortunately, that bands are at the mercy of club owners to get this needed exposure, and club owners know this and use it to their benefit. Not only will you probably not get paid (or paid next to nothing) you will be responsible for bringing in a good draw. In some clubs, if you don't bring in at least one hundred people, you'll never be booked again, let alone paid. Chances are you'll lose money on most gigs. Why?

Because you are responsible for the publicity, not the club. That means you have to mail out your own flyers or cards as well as distribute flyers or tickets around town.

▼ *What's the best way for a band to generate a following?*

To do this well, you have to develop a mailing list. The best idea is to print up a postcard that you can leave on every table in a club and anywhere else someone might pick it up. On the card write: "Get on (your band's name here) mailing list!" and leave ample space for people to write their address. Compile all these cards and add them to your list. These are, after all, people who have enjoyed your band enough to bother to fill out the card so they might also be willing to come to a future gig.

Then, every time you have a gig, mail out cards to everyone on the list at least three weeks prior to the date. Even if they don't come to each gig, in this way you'll be reminding them of the band's name and the fact that the band is currently gigging.

On your mailing list you should also put the name of every music reviewer or critic in your town. Again, they may never come to a single gig but they will begin to get familiar with the band and be aware that the band is performing regularly.

J. Michael Dolan, who is the publisher of Los Angeles' *Music Connection* magazine (one of the few publications in L.A. that reviews local bands), gave me this answer when I asked him what it took to get a review of a band. "If a band tells us they have one gig and it's this week, they won't get reviewed. However, if they send us something that says they have ten gigs in the next two or three months, they will get reviewed. You've got to give us the time and the opportunity to get there."

Once you get something in print about the band (remembering the old adage "no publicity is bad publicity") you can send photocopies of that blurb or story to other music writers, enabling them to see that there's a band in town others have written about and that is worth their attention. And hopefully, in time they'll pick up the lead and come and see you for themselves and write a review of the band. Each review you get will catch the attention of more people who might come out and see the band, and this is the beginning of a ''buzz.''

Once, when in a publisher's office, he listened to one of my tapes and said, ''This is great stuff. I love this. Don't know what to do with it, but I love it.'' With that he got on the phone, as publishers are wont to do in the middle of conversations, and called the main A&R person at one of the largest record companies in the world. ''Let's do lunch,'' he said to her and then mentioned having a kind of ''wacky, unusual project'' he wanted her to hear. I left that office, as I have left others, feeling I had finally arrived. All that was left, I believed, was for the lady to hear the tape and send over the contracts for me to sign. Of course, it didn't happen that way. She did like the tape, she told the publisher a few days later, but wasn't interested because there was no hype, no ''buzz'' about the band. I went back to work on my mailing list.

All of which goes to show that it takes more than ambition to launch a band or an artist these days. It takes a combination of performance ability, image, hype, willingness to be rejected, humility, and an enormous amount of persistence. More than anything, though, it depends on good songs. No matter what else you have going for you, if the songs aren't good, nothing else will matter.

Afterword

When getting involved in the business of songwriting with all of its licenses and royalties and percentages, it's easy to lose sight of the heart of this business: the song. Without an influx of new songs the music industry would grind to a halt. The need for new songs in the world is a constant one; as the world changes so does the need for different songs. There are still endless possibilities to be explored within the song itself and a profusion of unwritten songs yearning to be written.

The more time I've spent working on this book and conducting interviews about songwriting, the greater my hunger has become simply to return to the source, to writing songs. There's nothing that's more fun. It's a precious process and those of us lucky enough to have the time, talent, and inclination to become involved in this artform are in a privileged position; we're able to create universes out of words and music and enter them. As Van Dyke Parks said, "We create a world that we're subject to." They are worlds that are both spiritual and earthly simultaneously, speaking to the heart and mind at the same time.

Songs never age. Those that moved us when we were young retain their power, containing a fragment of eternity in the span of a few minutes. They are "little spirits" as Rickie Lee Jones called them, and they can change our lives if we let them. Jimmy Webb said, "I think even the most calloused among us feel that there is something timeless about this experience."

As we search for answers about songwriting we can read all the books we can find and talk to all the songwriters we can meet. But ultimately we come to the understanding that this is only a beginning, and that the real answers to our questions will only be found in the songs themselves.

Index

OTHER BOOKS TO HELP YOU MAKE
MONEY AND THE MOST OF
YOUR MUSIC TALENT

The Craft & Business of Songwriting
John Braheny

A powerful, information-packed (and the most up-to-date) book about the songwriting industry which thoroughly covers all the creative and business aspects that you need to know to maximize your chances of success. 322 pages/$19.95, hardcover

The Craft of Lyric Writing
Sheila Davis

Davis, a successful lyricist, composer, and teacher, presents the theory, principles, and techniques that result in lyrics with timeless appeal. 350 pages/$19.95, hardcover

Successful Lyric Writing:
A Step-by-Step Course & Workbook
Sheila Davis

A practical, self-contained lyric writing course, complete with exercises and lyric writing assignments designed to stimulate your creativity and build writing skills. 304 pages/$18.95, paperback

Getting Noticed:
A Musician's Guide to Publicity & Self-Promotion
James Gibson

Gibson helps performing musicians create effective yet inexpensive publicity materials, then use them to *get noticed* and *make money* with their music. 224 pages/$12.95, paperback

Making Money Making Music
(No Matter Where You Live)
James Dearing

Dearing shows you how to build a successful music career in any community—playing clubs, performing radio and TV jingles, operating a record studio, teaching, and selling lyrics through the mail. 305 pages/$12.95, paperback

The Performing Artist's Handbook
Janice Papolos

Practical know-how classical musicians need to progress in their professional music careers. 219 pages/ $12.95, paperback

The Songwriter's Guide to Making Great Demos
Harvey Rachlin

From how to judge if a song is ready to be pitched to exactly how to produce a multitrack recording, covers every step of the process of making great demos. 192 pages/$12.95, paperback

Writing Music for Hit Songs
Jai Josefs

Professional songwriter Jai Josefs shows how to musically craft successful popular songs. His easy-to-understand explanations are illustrated with more than 170 musical examples from today's top artists. 256 pages/$17.95, hardcover

Making It in the New Music Business
James Riordan

The coauthor of *The Platinum Rainbow* shows how to achieve success as a recording artist by building your own path to success. 377 pages/$18.95, hardcover

The Songwriter's Guide to Collaboration
Walter Carter
A complete guide to all aspects of co-writing songs, from working relationships to legal and financial arrangements. 178 pages/$12.95, paperback

How to Pitch & Promote Your Songs
Fred Koller
For songwriters who want to make a full-time living with their music, a step-by-step self-employment guide. 144 pages/$12.95, paperback

You Can Write Great Lyrics
Pamela Phillips Oland
Inside advice from one of today's top songwriters on how you can write lyrics with commercial appeal and focus on writing songs that have what it takes to succeed. 192 pages/$17.95, paperback

Protecting Your Songs & Yourself
Kent J. Klavens
A practical, thorough, easy-to-read guide to copyright, contracts, taxes, and other songwriting legal topics. 112 pages/$15.95, paperback

Playing for Pay:
How to Be a Working Musician
James Gibson
Gibson shows you how to develop a well-organized and strategic "Personal Music Marketing System" that will help you make money with your music. 160 pages/$17.95, paperback

Beginning Songwriter's Answer Book
Paul Zollo
An essential resource for songwriters, with detailed answers to the 218 questions most often asked the National Academy of Songwriters. 128 pages/$16.95, paperback

Gigging:
The Musician's Underground Touring Directory
Michael Dorf & Robert Appel
2,000 contacts to help you/your group book a regional or cross-country tour and/or get airplay for your records. 224 pages/$14.95, paperback

1990 Songwriter's Market
edited by Mark Garvey
This annual directory is designed to help you make the right contacts! Includes 2,000 listings of music publishers, record companies/producers, advertising agencies, audiovisual firms, managers, booking agents, and play producers. You'll also find helpful articles on the business of songwriting, interviews with professionals in the industry, and lists of clubs, contests, and associations. 528 pages/$18.95, hardcover

A complete catalog of all Writer's Digest Books is available FREE by writing to the address shown below. To order books directly from the publisher, include $3.00 postage and handling for one book, 50¢ for each additional book. Allow 30 days for delivery.

Writer's Digest Books
1507 Dana Avenue
Cincinnati, Ohio 45207

Credit card orders call TOLL-FREE
1-800-289-0963

Prices subject to change without notice